A Song at Bedtime

By Nell Parsons

A Family Story
1889 – 1990

Memories of Mum and Dad

Published by New Generation Publishing in 2013

Copyright © Nell Parsons 2013

First Edition

The author asserts the moral right under the Copyright, Designs and Patents Act 1988 to be identified as the author of this work.

All Rights reserved. No part of this publication may be reproduced, stored in a retrieval system or transmitted, in any form or by any means without the prior consent of the author, nor be otherwise circulated in any form of binding or cover other than that which it is published and without a similar condition being imposed on the subsequent purchaser.

www.newgeneration-publishing.com

 New Generation Publishing

Acknowledgements

In the writing of this story I wish to pay special thanks to the following in providing me with the information, help and support.

Firstly to Elsie, Jack and our dear late brother Leonard for their assistance in helping me to remember things that I had forgotten, as well as for getting my facts correct.

Special thanks also to our late cousin Clarence Opie Nicholls for all his hard work in researching the Nicholls, Opie and Martin family tree and passing this information onto me.

Finally, a very special thanks to my darling daughter Maureen, for all the help and encouragement she gave me, as well as the nagging, without which I would never have finished this story.

Index of Chapters

Chapter 1   **The childhood of Mum and Dad**

Chapter 2   **The Marriage of William John and Amelia (Amy) Jones**

Chapter 3   **The Depression of the 1930's**

Chapter 4   **The Start of World War II**

Chapter 5   **After the War**

Chapter 6   **Mum's life without Dad**

The Nicholls Family Tree

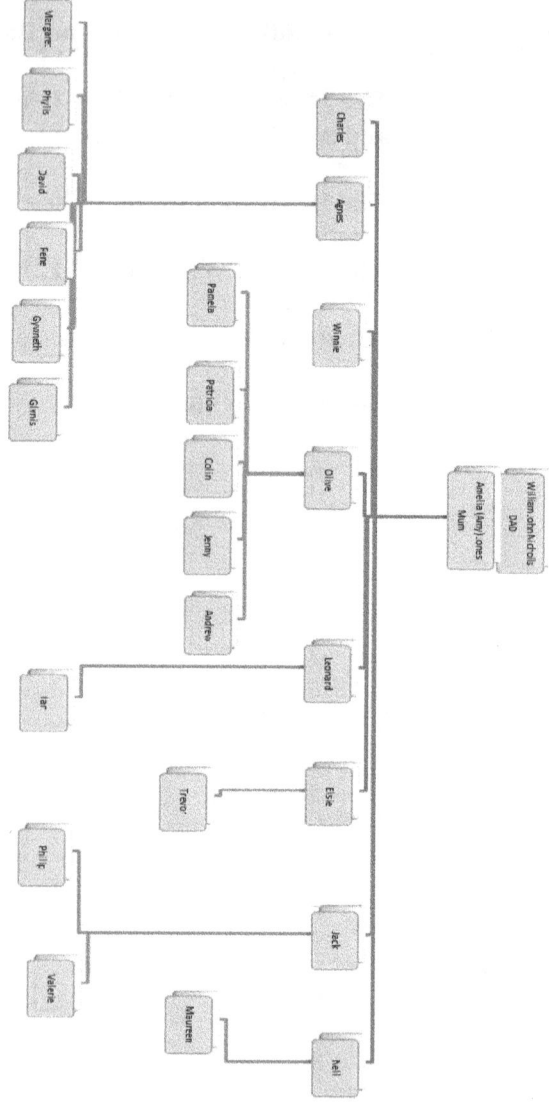

Mum, on her 88th Birthday
With Five of her Children
Jack, Mum, Nell, Agnes, Elsie, Len

Mum & Dad
Len
Elsie & Jack
1934

Agnes & Mum
1934, Hadleigh

Mum Holding
Baby Phylli
Nell 1934

The cover photo is of Nell with mum in 1933 on Southend Beach.

The gas mask photo is of Dad preparing for war in 1939 distributing gas masks.

The party photo is of the London Evacuees Christmas Party in Penzance 1940 that Dad helped organise

Mum & Dad
Baby Agnes
1913

Mum's four eldest, Olive, Agnes
Holding baby Leonard, & Winnie

Baby Olive,
Born 1919

Leonard David and Baby Elsie Irene
Born 1922 & 1924

Mum, Dad and Baby Nell
Born 1929

Foreword

I have chosen the title 'A Song at Bedtime', because as children, and even up to the time we all left home, music and singing was part of the everyday ritual in our family especially at bedtime. The songs we sang around the fireplace on winter evenings were reminiscences of songs mum and dad had learnt at the old time music halls when they were young.

In writing this brief resume of my parents, I hope that to the now only two remaining of my siblings it will bring back some laughs and happy memories of their childhood, also to those of their grandchildren who remember them, and who shared some of these times. More importantly to those of the grandchildren, great grandchildren, and great great grandchildren who sadly never knew them, but who will hopefully appreciate that they were descended from, a poor, but rich, in that it was a very loving family.

Love Nell

October 2013

Chapter One

The Childhood of Mum and Dad

William John Nicholls

William was born on the 28th of October 1889, in Camberwell Street, Penzance in Cornwall. (It was just around the corner from his Grandfather Edward Nicholls house, from where he ran his shoemaker's business). His Father was Charles Nicholls, master house painter, and his mother was Agnes Nicholls (nee Opie). Agnes on her mother's side was the granddaughter of Ann Martin, where we can trace the family back to 1578. William was the second child and first son of Charles and Agnes.

Charles's mother was the great granddaughter of a soldier, David Davies, who was in the Welsh Fusiliers during the Napoleonic war in the year 1797. Charles himself would put on a uniform in his spare time, to play in the Penzance silver band.

The house where he was born was set in a pretty little road with just enough room for a single small horse and carriage to drive up.

It was one of ten terraced houses, there were ten more exactly the same opposite. They each had a small walled garden in the front, with a gate leading to the front door, which led straight into the front parlour, which was usually kept for visitors. Behind the front parlour, was another parlour, with a door to the side, behind which, was a staircase, leading up to the two bedrooms. Behind the back parlour was a leanto that contained a washboiler and a sink. William's mother was able to do all her washing out there. Before

Grandma could do her washing, she would first have to prepare the soap. This would be a hard piece of usually Sunlight Soap. She had to shave off enough to do her washing. Once that was done, she would then place it, plus a handful of washing soda, into the boiling water, stir it all around until the soap had melted, then she could start her wash day. The cooking range was situated in the back parlour. As well as having a small front garden each house had a walled back yard, and had its own privy, instead of being shared with a few more families, as so many were in the eighteen eighties. Apparently the street used to win the prize each year for the prettiest gardens in Penzance.

There would be three more children to complete the family, but by this time the enlarged family would have moved into a larger house in the next road, Mount Street.

Many years later his eldest daughter Agnes Emma would be born at the same house in Mount Street.

Unfortunately before William was eight years of age his father died, leaving his mother a widow with five children.

William's youngest sister Emmaline Chappel Nicholls was born after the death of Charles Nicholls, Williams father. Emmaline's father was a cousin of William's father (Mr Chappell). On a visit from America, he met Grandma, and wanted to marry her, which she agreed to do. She became pregnant with Emmaline, but then discovered that he only wanted her and not her five older children as well. The marriage did not take place, but she gave the baby her father's surname as her middle name. According to the research undertaken by Cousin Clarence this was common practice at that time. Mr Chappel sailed off into the sunset back to America.....

William went to St Johns Church of England School, where he was a very good scholar and would repeatedly win the top prize. *(Many years later his teacher met my mother, and told her that he was her little ray of sunshine, which caused my mother to laugh and tease him ever after).* He had a beautiful singing voice and was a chorister in the local church. His sister Jane would remark in later years that when people knew that he was going to sing solo, the church would be packed.

At this time, Truro Cathedral was in the process of being built. The first foundation stones being laid in 1887, two years before William was born. Cornwall at that time was part of the Diocese of Exeter, it was said that twice he took the Prize back to Cornwall for best boy chorister, and he was offered a place in the Cathedral boy's school, but unfortunately his mother wouldn't allow him to go. According to what was known, 'Grandma' had said *"what was good for one was good for them all"*. It was a wonderful opportunity sadly missed. One can only assume that they were choosing the chorister's for the new Cathedral in Truro, which was finally completed in 1910, but services were already being held in the partly built church before the final completion.

Soon after, William ran away to sea, at the very young age of thirteen. It was thought that this may be due to the severe disappointment he must have felt. In running away, he wouldn't have been equipped with enough warm clothing to face the cold weather, which would lie ahead; his first trip being to Russia. He must have been a very determined young boy.

We don't know how long he stayed away, but on his return from sea, William worked in the office at one of the local tin mines as a pay clerk. But the sea was in his blood, and forever after, he would take off to sea. He always kept his seaman's ticket, and when jobs became hard to get ashore, if a ship was available off he would go.

Apparently one of the first songs he ever sang in public was *"In the Shade of The Old AppleTree"*, and people made a collection and gave him money, which he took home and gave to his mother. The family remained in Mount Street, Penzance until the 1930's.

Amelia Nicholls, (Amy) nee Jones

Amy was born in Chancery Lane Canton Cardiff, on 28th December 1892. She was the first child, and only daughter of William Jones, Journeyman Master Boiler Maker, and Margaret Jones (nee Sullivan). Her brother, John (Uncle Jack) would be born eighteen months later. She was born into a happy home with lots of aunts, uncles, and cousins some being the same age as herself as well as her brother Jack.

Both her grandparents, on her mother's side were Irish, and on her father's side Welsh. In fact her paternal grandmother hardly spoke any English, Welsh being the first Language in her home. Her Granny Martha was born in St. Dogarths in Wales. Her father was William Davis, and he was a Grocer. Amy was christened and confirmed at St Mary's Catholic Cathedral in Cardiff. However, on Sundays, her welsh grandmother, would take her to her church (Welsh Baptist), where the service would be completely conducted in the welsh language. She loved her grandmother (Granny Martha), very much, and would spend an awful lot of time at her house, where she would have young aunts and uncles to spoil her.

Mum used to say that her father would sit her on his

knee and sing a little song that he'd made up, "Amelia was pretty, Amelia was fair, and she lived with her Granny in Mount Stuart Square". Mum also used to recall how at that time there used to be an advertisement for 'Mazawattee Tea', showing an old lady with a little girl. Mum's granny, used to tell her; "now Amy that is you and me". Years later we were to find a reproduction of the advertisement, which now hangs on my kitchen wall.

Her father had a very good job, repairing and fitting ships boilers when steam was a new innovation. She remembered that when her father was called away to do repairs on the ship's boilers abroad, he would always bring home gifts for her and her brother, especially if he went to France.

One time she recalled, after being away, he arrived home in a hansom cab with a big doll for her and a rocking horse for her little brother. Another lovely gift she had was the forerunner of the gramophone, the records were cylindrical in shape and they had great fun listening to it. The family would frequently go on the ferry for day trips to Weston (Weston-Super-Mare). They would also go away on family holidays. Sometimes the whole family would be taken to the theatre, but more often to the music halls. The songs she learnt there she would later teach her children.

The family would also all go off on picnics. Her aunt Polly, (her father's sister), kept a Pub, the 'Crown and Sceptre'. It was she, who would hire the brewers dray, and borrow benches from the church, which were placed down either side of the dray. In the centre would be placed a coal brazier, filled with sticks and coal all ready to be lit, plus a spare bucket of coal. The food and drink would all be set down in the centre of the dray.

The men would have small barrels of beer to drink, and the ladies and children would have ginger beer, Dandelion & Burdock, plus water, and little muslin bags filled with loose tea, and all kinds of goodies to eat such as; meat pies, sausage rolls, cold chicken, sandwiches and lots of cakes. To provide the music they would take concertina and a banjo, a pair of spoons, and a comb with a piece of paper wrapped around it, and off they would all go. They would arrive back home, tired, grubby, and very happy after a wonderful day out. Maybe that was the forerunner of today's BBQ.

She also remembered the time when her mother had decided, that her father was spending too much time over at Aunt Polly's Pub. She sent Amy over with a duster and some polish, with the instruction's to tell her father that, as he was spending so much time sitting his backside down on aunt Polly's chairs, he may as well polish them at the same time

As small children they had great fun playing in the Coal Exchange. The Coal Exchange was situated in Mount Stuart Square, opposite where her Granny Jones lived in a large three-story house. Amy and her brother were allowed to run around in the Coal Exchange as one of her aunt's was at that time engaged to one of the young men who worked in one of the offices there. Unfortunately this aunt died before they were married. He was later to become Lord Glenealy.

Whilst living in Mount Stuart Square, her father employed a maid named Mary, to help her mother who at that time was unwell. She would say that both she and her brother would go up to Mary's room, where they had a lovely view of the ships in the docks. They could see their parents return in a Hansom cab after a night out. Once her father for a dare swam from one side of the docks, to the other side, with a flagon of beer in each coat pocket, of course he won the bet.

Her father was also the captain of one of the local Rugby clubs. His nickname was 'Doggie Jones'. *(It may well have been 'Dodgy Jones', if he was any good at getting the ball through the scrum).* For years after she would search through published photos of Cardiff's rugby clubs hoping to find his picture amongst them. She remembered seeing one, when she was a child, but unfortunately she had lost the only photo of her father that she had.

Amelia was thirteen years of age when her world fell apart. After a long illness, her mother died. Six months later she found her father dead in his bed. They told her that her father had died of a broken heart; he had grieved so much after loosing their mother. By this time of course they had also lost both of their grandparents. Their lives would have been so very different, if her Granny Jones had still been alive.

She and her brother were together for a little while; staying first of all with her mother's sister, (Julia), who had several children. All her children were boys. They were known as Mr. and Mrs. Chick. *Mum would always shudder when she spoke of them, and said he was a 'horrible man'.* However, an aunt from the Jones's side of the family went to visit them, and found Amelia scrubbing the aunt's floors. The visiting aunt packed Amelia's bags and took her away; telling everybody that *"Amelia wasn't brought up to scrub anyone's floors!"* And so she and her brother were separated, and didn't see each other very much after that. And all this by the time she was fourteen.

Their father had left them pretty comfortably off, as well as his money; they were also given money from the boilermaker's union, to help with their education. They were allowed £4 pounds a month each towards their education and their upkeep, until the age of twenty one, when they would have been entitled to whatever remained of the trust. Uncles from both sides of the family were acting as executors of his will, and it would appear, that there was a bit of conflict between the two families. Both sides, each were trying to do their best for these orphaned children and neither side succeeding. Her Aunt Polly, who had two children already in a boarding school wanted to send both of them as well, but that was not to be allowed. So she and her brother Jack hardly saw each other, both living with different sides of the family.

The only job that she had was in ladies outfitters, in the centre of Cardiff. At that time in her life, she lived with a member of her father's family the Morgans, she and their daughter Minnie, were very good friends and they remained friends for many years. In fact we children, when we were small would always refer to them as uncle Clem and 'Nanny Morgan'. She would remain with that family until her marriage, to William John Nicholls.

Amelia was to meet her future husband William through her uncle Clem, apparently they worked together, and William was in lodgings close by. *I suppose it's hard for us to imagine both Mum and Dad being young.* They would go off to the theatre, the music halls, dancing, and cycle riding. William (Will) was a lovely dancer, Very light on his feet. *Later on he would teach both Elsie and me to dance, he would be very strict on posture our backs had to be straight and our heads held high. I can remember both our parents dancing in a church hall at a Christmas party.*

As for the bike, I can recall seeing dad on a bike, and shouting for mum to came and see. Although he could ride a bike, he couldn't stop it. He would slow down and head for the nearest tree or lamppost, where he would be able to wrap one arm around which ever came first the tree or lamppost. We kids would think it a huge joke, and mum after a lot of tut tutting would say "you'll fall of and break your blooming neck one of these days" but all he would say in his Cornish brogue was, "well I haven't done it yet me dearrr". And he would have a laugh at himself.

Years later; Amy with her sister-in-law 'Cissy' (Cecelia, married to Amy's brother Jack) decided to visit an uncle and aunt of Amelia's with their new babies; Agnes and Eric, who lived in a very select part of Cardiff. When they knocked at the front door, a maid greeted them. The maid invited them in and proceeded to get the mistress of the house. Cissy gazed around the hall, looking at the furnishings and fittings. When she arrived Cissy said to the aunt, 'what a lovely home you have, on my husband's and his sister's money!!' I don't think they were ever invited back!

Chapter Two

The Marriage of William John And Amelia (Amy) Jones

William and Amy (Amelia) were married on the 13th of March in the 1913.

The marriage would take place in Cardiff. At the registrar's office, none of her family it appears attended her marriage, Uncle Clem was her only witness, and it would appear that he gave permission for the marriage, as she was still under age at the time.

Apparently she had gone to one of her uncles to ask for his permission, and also for an advance of her allowance as she wanted to marry, but he refused both request's, saying that she would have to wait until she was twenty-one. At which point she told him exactly what he could do with her money and it would appear that he did, *(a trait that some of her children and a few of her grandchildren would pick up.)* Strange that on the marriage certificate dad had put himself down as a Labourer, what sort of labouring one can only make a guess at, as we never knew him to lift a shovel in his life!

The reason mum went to her uncle for money was that both her parents died within six months of each other, leaving her brother and her orphans. This was the money left by her father and the boilermakers union in trust for them.

Their first child was born prematurely in 1913, a little boy who was named Charles after his paternal grandfather. He was a very poorly baby, and mum said that both she and dad would walk up and down the room trying to soothe his crying, he was a

Hydrocephalic, hence all the crying. Sadly he passed away soon after.

Their second child Agnes Emma was also born prematurely in 1914, in Mount Street, Penzance. She only weighed 4lbs and mum and Granny Nicholls wrapped her in cotton wool and placed her in a little crib close to the range and fed her on 'Virol' and snips of Brandy. Fortunately, she survived, and when she was strong enough they took her back to Wales.

At this time dad was in the army, it was during the First World War. He was a Recruiting Sergeant in "The Royal Horse Artillery". His base was in Snowdonia and that is where, mum took her baby Agnes to live. She would say how beautiful it was. With baby Agnes in her arms she was able to gaze out of her bedroom window to Snowdonia. It was also during this time, that dad saw action and was injured at Gallipoli. It was in this battle that dad was reported missing. Mum took both Agnes and the new baby, Margaret Winnifred, (Winnie) and off they went to stay with grandma in Cornwall, It was quite a while before they discovered that dad was lying injured in a foreign hospital.

Dad's grandmother, known by us as Granny Underwood; *(her name being Ann Underwood nee Opie)* was living with Grandma. Every month she would take herself off to Falmouth, to visit her sister, but also to collect her pension. Her last employer left the pension to her, when she retired. She was employed as a housekeeper in a large estate. Apparently, she was very Victorian in her manner, and everything had to be just right. She had tea at precisely four o - clock with her own bone china tea set, and if she didn't have the first cup of tea out of the pot, grandma would have to make a fresh one. Mum said she led grandma a dog's life. However she would demand that Agnes and Winifred visit her, and she gave them their pocket money, a penny a week. So she couldn't have been all-bad. Dad was finally found, so mum, and the two little girls went home back to Cardiff, where Olive and Leonard were born. The children came along every couple of years, Margaret Winifred in 1916; Olive Emmaline, 1919; Leonard David 1922; the last three all being born in Cardiff.

Mum said that this was one of the best times of her life to have all her lovely babies around her, and one can understand how she must have felt; having had such an unhappy time since her parents had died. At this moment in time, dad had a good job being under manager in a large hotel, so much so that they were able to send Agnes just before the age of five, to a private school. They lived in a nice house where the three little girls were dressed alike in cotton pinafore dresses with frilly white aprons which um had made for them, and big bows of ribbon in their hair. They also helped to take care of their baby brother, Leonard David who according to mum was dressed practically the same, but without the frilly apron! They also attended to their own little bits of garden. known as, Agnes' *'Love Garden'*, as all the flowers that she grew, were either; *'Love-in-a-mist'* or *'Love-lies-bleeding'*, and *'forget-me-knots'*. The other two grew vegetables. Mum always talked of Agnes and her *'Bleeding Hearts'!* At that time they were a happy little family of six.

This happy period in their lives was about to change. In 1921 one year before Len was born, the country was far into the Red, and suddenly there were two million unemployed. It didn't have any effect on mum and dad for another couple of years, when I suppose, like everyone else they thought things could only get better. However dad suddenly found himself one of the two million people unemployed, but after a while he managed to find work in London.

Dad's new job meant the family had to move to Greenwich, they were fortunate in being able to do so. The situation was far worse in Wales, and the North of the country, as the coal mines and the mills were closing down, many men had to leave their wives and children behind, whilst they searched for work anywhere in the country. In one respect mum and dad were lucky in being able to stay together.

Dad was employed, by a local Authority, dealing with people, on what they called in those days, "Poor Relief ". These were people, who because of the depression, all over the country, were unable to find work. They and their families, needed to be fed and the children clothed, to enable them to go to school. There was no such thing as unemployment benefit, way back then, and with no money coming in they would have to apply to the 'Relieving Office', for new clothes, shoes, and food tickets etc. Some were lucky enough to be allocated to dad, who would go to their homes to assess them as to their needs. Mum would say years later, that he was too soft. Dad would hand out all the necessary tickets, for the children's needs, plus bedding. It was a choice, either the Local Authority became broke, or Dad would have to go, which he did. They did say that the people would later sell the clothes for cash, so unfortunately the children would still go to school barefooted. Still they had to eat, and it was better to have food on the table than shoes on your feet.

The situation was desperate. In 1926 the country was in the throes of a general strike. Millions out of work, no money coming in, and the people were finding it very hard just to survive. They were still moving all around the country, seeking jobs where they could, even if only for a couple of days.

With no money coming in dad's own family had to

survive, so, he did the only job he knew, he went back to sea. This allowed mum to have a small allowance coming in, and although heavily pregnant with William John, 'Jack'. For the first time in her married life, she went out to work, washing for the soldiers in the local barracks. My elder sisters would later recall that time. Spending hours over the huge tubs, mum could hardly straighten her back, so they would wheel Len and Elsie in their pram down to meet her and to help her home. Thank goodness dad wasn't away for too long, as she only did that for a short while. It was around about this time in their lives, that they were to face further anxieties.

Leonard became very ill with Double Pneumonia and Pleurisy; he was only four years old still very young. They both spent as much time as was allowed in the hospital. Visiting time was usually only twice a week, in the afternoons for one hour. When he was able to come home, the whole family went as well. Dad carried him through the streets on his shoulder. People would remark what a beautiful child he was, and call him *'Bubbles'*. With his head full of golden curls he was very reminiscent of a painting, by Sir Joshua Reynolds called *'Bubbles'*. Len still remembered dad carrying him into the local army barracks and sitting him on the horse's back's, then taking him for a treat of toast with dripping and a cup of tea. A rare treat indeed especially when money was in short supply. Len also recalled an occasion his older sisters taking him down to the docks, where he promptly fell in. But dad being close by, quickly lay down on his stomach and grabbed him by his hair to pull him out. Len used to say he could still remember all the green slime on the dock wall.

It was still a very worrying time for everyone, as jobs were still very hard to come by. Luckily dad still had his seaman's ticket, and would get a ship, whenever possible. We had lost about a third of our Merchant fleet by this time, being unable to replace the ships lost during *The Great War'* '. Although mum appreciated the little bit of money coming in, she found it really hard being left with no family around her, other than her six children to care for. By this time William John, (Jack) had arrived; he was born in 1926, two years after Elsie Irene,

I can well remember one day, when dad was out. We were sitting around the fireplace, and mum was talking to us about her problems. Dad arrived home and immediately asked her, not to discuss her problems with the children, they would have enough problems of their own when they grew up he said. She never did again, unless we asked her. I suppose with dad being away so much she was used to talking things over with us her children.

It was around this time, when Agnes would become very ill, with Tapeworm (a parasite that invades the intestine). She was only thirteen and mum was on her own. Dad being away, and with the other children, to care for, things were very difficult, Jack being still a baby. Winnie being the next eldest, with Olive helping her, was left in charge of the other three, while mum spent as much time as possible in the hospital with Agnes. She was so ill; mum thought she was going to lose her. She was in hospital quite a while, and when she was ready to come home mum wanted her to go down to granny's in Cornwall to convalesce, however Grandma wrote back to say that it wasn't convenient. As young as she was, Olive never forgave grandma for not helping mum when she needed it.

Olive would later tell me all about this story, more than thirty years after the event.

However, Agnes was able to get away for a holiday.

She went to Kent, and mum would travel all the way to Kent to visit her. That in itself was quite a feat, as in those days it was a very long journey, and must have been very worrying for her, having to leave the rest of the children, back home in the care of Winnie and Olive. Life went on after all that worry, and when she felt less tired, mum would take all the children to the park to play.

Some of the parks had little zoo's in them with tropical birds, and different species of ducks and swans and the usual swings. They would take their sandwiches and bottles of lemonade, and spend the summer afternoons playing in the park. Dad arrived home, and still worrying about Agnes, they came to the decision to move out of London,

The General strike was just beginning to get nasty, with marchers waving banners they seemed to be everywhere. The people were getting desperate for work, and for better living conditions. So mum and dad decided to move out into the country. By this time in 1930, they would have had their last child, born in 1929, Nellie Doreen, (me) and settled in the Benfleet and Hadliegh area.

When I was born mum had developed Eclampsia a life threatening condition of pregnancy, *(a condition that a few years later on, our sister Winnie would also have and lose her life and that of her baby)*. However to come to my birth; Eclampsia causes the mother to have high blood pressure and fits, and I was born during one of mum's fits. The doctor asked my father who should he save, naturally the choice was my mother, but I survived, *(and lived happily ever after). I would also have the same condition, when I got married and having my children. My first daughter survived, (prematurely), but unfortunately, her little sister died. I'm mentioning all this, because there is a possibility it may run in the family, as one of mother's great-granddaughters was to experience the same problem.*

There was more work to be had around that area, because of all the barges coming down from London, laden with all the waste and garbage. They were rebuilding the docks in between Canvey and Benfleet. A lot of mums' countrymen seeking work had made their way down from Wales and most of them being ex-miners were ideal for the job. They would have been experienced in the timberwork, needed for building and shoring up the new docks.

Naturally they needed places to live, and in those days many people took in lodgers (or as the posh people would say 'paying guest's'). However, mum and dad took in a couple of lodgers. Len and Jack thought they were great fun, and would go off down to the river to watch them at work. When the men stopped work, and before coming home, they would stop off, at one of the pubs for a drink, and if the boys were around, they would have a treat of lemonade, or an arrowroot biscuit. They were huge things, twice the size and twice as thickness of a normal biscuit.

By this time, both Agnes and Winnie had jobs, each of them looking after children. After work they would do what most teenagers would do at that time, although they used to say, that dad was very strict, and they would have to be in by nine-o-clock at the latest. When we younger ones were growing up, they reckon that we got away with murder. One of Agnes best friends then was a girl whose father ran a pub called 'The Crown and Anchor', her name was Ivy.

Olive, Len, and Elsie were all at school. That left just Jack and me at home for a little while longer. When Jack was just five years old, his big brother Len took him to school along with Elsie. They would all have to wait for each other and all come home together. I can also remember our sister Winnie, if we happened to be in the toilet, she would call out to us through the door *"I hope you're not eating anything while you're in there? If you are, it's going straight to the devil." Still to this day my sister Elsie and I look down the loo, to make sure the devil isn't lurking down in the depths of the toilet bowl!!*

It was whilst we were living here in Benfleet, that Len would have the job of going over to the farm nearby to collect the milk. *(Maybe this is where my sister Olive met her future husband Jim, as he worked on the farm. He told me in later years, that he and Olive would wheel me around in my pushchair. So she would only have been around twelve at that time.)* However going back to the milk, the milkmen would deliver their milk in their horse and carts. The milk would be in large silver metal containers, and they would have all the measuring ladles, with long handles hanging from the sides of the milk churns. The milkmen would ring a loud bell and call out *"milk-oh.!!"* Housewives or the children would go out with their jugs, or grey metal containers with lids attached to collect the milk.

Later on the milk would be delivered by the milkman pulling an electric buggy; it was square shaped with along handle in the front. The milkman would release the hand brake and walk along pulling his cart. On arriving at his next customer, he would stop, put on the handbrake, and deliver his milk. *(The practise of delivering milk with a horse and cart and the milk churns went on for a number of years. The last one we can recall was about the latter part of the 1950's. Phillips Dairy in West Road Prittlewell sold out to the larger firm, of Howards Dairy. They would still use the horse and cart, but of course by that time, the milk would be in bottles. Philips Dairyman would be dressed in thick trousers, strong leather gaiters, white coat and a bowler hat.)* One hates to think what would have happened, if he had stopped on a hill, and forgot to put on his handbrake.

It was around this time that Agnes was to meet her future husband; he was a Welshman from the Rhondda Valley in Wales, and an ex-miner. His name was Edward James Adlam (Ted). His cousin Charlie Morris was one of our lodgers. After the dock work had finished, Ted worked on building the engine house for the sewerage works, which is still situated in Rushbottom Lane Benfleet, alongside the the unpretentious building that replaced it.

We lived at that time quite near the main London road. During the summer there would be loads of coaches driving through, filled with the girls and boys who worked in the factories in the East End of London. Such as 'Bryant & Mays' the matchmakers, and 'Tate & Lyle' the sugar and jam manufacturers, 'Weston's' the biscuit makers, plus many others. They would all be on their way to Southend-on-Sea for a days outing. The girls dressed in their pretty summer dresses; the boys and the men in grey flannel trousers, with white shirts and usually fancy waistcoats, or pullovers all heading for a good time at the seaside, and a paddle.

It would be quite a long journey, and they would make a few stops along the way, to lubricate their vocal cords; one of them being the 'Tarpots Pub' a few minutes from where we lived. Mum used to say, that she and Agnes would go and watch all the coaches coming in, and be really entertained at all the antics, the visitors would get up too. They liked it so much, that they both got a job, looking after the ladies loo in the 'Tarpots Pub', they earnt quite a bit of money doing this, plus enjoying themselves at the same time.

Dad also had his own cockle stall outside the pub. The cockles came from Leigh. The fishermen would put the cockles in baskets, on the train at Leigh station, and Len would have to go down to Benfleet station to collect them, plus take the empty baskets back, and put them on the train to be picked up at Leigh station. Maybe he used my old pram, as I don't think he had a barrow. One can only imagine them all having a lovely time there, it's a pity it only lasted during the summer months

A couple of years later Grandma came for a visit from Penzance in Cornwall, and after living in that small fishing place, when dad took her down to the town in Southend, she got so frightened dad had to bring her back home. I don't believe she ever made it to the seafront.

During the summer, Southend was a very lively place, always crowds of people here for the day or on holiday. The boarding houses and the hotels, would be packed, so much so, that people would even sleep under the pier. When you walked down the high street, and made your way down towards the sea front, it would be so full of people, you could have stood still and the crowd would have carried you along. When you did finely reach the sea front, it would seem to be worse. The pubs would be so full, they would all be drinking outside, and the beer would be passed over their heads. The smells of the beer, and the sausage's, and onion's cooking in the window, of a restaurant on the pier hill, Fish and chips shops galore, Cockles and Whelks; people eating them out of little white dishes with loads of vinegar and pepper on them. It really was a beehive of a place. There would be several busker's, and men standing on small wooden pulpits, shouting about politics, the state of the country, and their various religious beliefs, and everything else they didn't feel was right *(according to them),* about the state of the world. One of these characters was, a chap called 'Happy Harry'. He would rant and rave about religion and hellfire, the stories being relayed at the time were that the young men would torment the poor man and heat up pennies with their cigarette lighters, and of course as he picked up the coins he would burn his fingers,' *how's that for a bit of hellfire they would shout with laughter '!!*

Another story that was frequently told at the time was how one year when the girls from the match factory were down for their usual day trip; something was said by 'Happy Harry' and they chased him on to the mud and they stripped him of all his clothes, and left them piled up on the promenade. It doesn't need too much of ones imagination, to imagine the scene; of matronly ladies, and people sitting down in their deck chairs enjoying the sea breeze; children with their buckets and spades playing on the sand; suddenly, seeing poor 'Harry' stark naked, rushing across the mud to retrieve his clothing. One could have a wonderful time and be entertained whilst walking along the prom on a summer day, and all for free. At this moment in time I am of cause talking of the nineteen thirties.

Agnes and Ted were married at Southend Registrar Office in 1932. Their first child Margaret Rose was also born in that year. Mum and dads, first grandchild, and the apple of their eye. When Ted came back from the hospital and told them the news, mums first reaction was to run outside to tell the first person she saw that she was now a granny. Well she did just that, and he happened to be a policeman. Poor bloke was surprised to have this lady rush up to him, and throw her arms around his neck, and say, *'I'm a Granny.'* Strangely enough Margaret's eldest son was to grow up to be a policeman. Agnes and Ted were living with us at the time, and so a larger house was needed, and we moved up to Hadleigh. Agnes and Ted were able to live in two rooms in the house next door to ours. Agnes would take her baby Margaret to the baby clinic, in Hadleigh where she won a first prize, and given a silver spoon, for *'bonniest baby'* in the clinic

Of course the lodgers came as well, and by this time the family would be enlarged still further. Ted's sister Lillian (Lil) would be living with us, she had been working in London and had come down for a visit, and decided to stay.

Olive left school, and with Winnie and Lil, went to work at the Salvation Army colony in Hadleigh, Picking fruit and vegetables. Winnie also had a little job helping a lady who they said was a 'Russian Princess', a refugee from the Russian Revolution. She loved animals, and Winnie would go and help her sometimes. She became very friendly with mum and her young family, and one story that was told was how our cat became unwell, and this lady would send over tins of red Salmon for the cat's tea. Well you can imagine, with all that family, tins of red Salmon were a luxury only for visitors, or for tea on rare occasions, not for our cat, they made lovely salmon and cucumber sandwiches for our tea.

These were really halcyon days for mum and dad, all the family in work, plus the lodgers, the four youngest children all at school, and all the family fit and well. The house where we lived was quite nice, semi-detached with lots of spare land all around us, lots of room for we children to play in safety. Much to Jack's delight, there were also plenty of orchard's to go scrumping in. He was only seven at this time, and he would practically roll up the road with apples or plums stuffed up his jumper. He was rather a sturdily built little boy, and with the sight of him rolling up the road with this heavy load stuffed up his jumper, mum couldn't tell him off, as she would be laughing too much.

In the summertime Winnie, Olive, and Lil would be out on the front lawn with their gramophone, playing their records singing and dancing to the popular songs of their day. *"Oh play to me gypsy", "Alexander's Ragtime Band"* The *'White Gardenia'* and others. When Agnes was newly married, and still living at home, she apparently would go around the house singing *"You are my hearts delight",* until one day mum told her to be quiet, or she would throw something at her. Well poor Agnes, being in love thought she would chance her luck, and kept on singing, until a pan came flying through the air, mums aim was so good, that she always missed. Another time apparently, she threw a big bag of flour at someone, also an opened tin of condensed milk, thankfully not all at the same time. I would have hated to be around helping to clear that lot up. No wonder they would say, *"Watch out Mum's got her Irish up".* She'd be like one of Nelsons battle ships in full sail!

On Saturday evenings mum, dad, Agnes and Ted would all go off to Southend for the evening leaving Winnie and Olive in charge of all the younger children. That was fine until mum and dad discovered that the girls had invited their friends in to party, and had been drinking. The discovery was made, by mum and dad, due to my older sisters not knowing what to do with the empty wine bottles. Being full of initiative they had made a big slit in the back of the settee and stuffed it with their empty bottles. Of course, when the settee was moved all you could here was the sound of empty bottles rattling around.

Agnes' husband Ted, was given a greyhound, called *'Shenigo'*, which he kept in our back garden. He would take great pride in this dog, and you can imagine his delight when he was asked to take it up to the local dog track, which was, at that time the top of the Rayleigh Road, *(where Sainsbury's supermarket is now situated.)* So off he went, with all of his mates on this Saturday evening, talking about how much money they were going to place on *'Shenigo'*, and how much money Ted would make, as the owner. Everyone was eagerly waiting for them to arrive back home, when they did eventually appear, the men were all laughing and happy which raised everyone's hopes thinking about their winnings. They said the dog had won, and they were all going out to celebrate. The celebrations went on until people started asking about their winnings, then Ted and his mates had to confess about what actually had happened. It appears that Ted placed *'Shenigo'* into the trap with the other dogs. He then stood to one side with his mates. The hare started to come round the track, gathering speed. As it neared the dog traps, the traps all opened, out came all the dogs, and off they went chasing after the hare, all with the exception of *'Shenigo'*, who promptly came and sat down alongside Ted, and watched all the other dogs racing. Having the dog was a better hobby for Ted, than his previous one. He had bought an old motorbike, he couldn't ride. But never the less after work, he would get his motor bike out, and sit on the saddle. The boys would give him a push, and off he would go, freewheeling down *'Bread and Cheese Hill'* with the kids running along side. Once down the hill, they would help him push it all the way back, and the whole exercise would start over again. It was a good job that in those days there wasn't too much traffic on the roads. At the time Ted had *'Shenigo'*; one of the lodgers had a 'French Cockerel'. Arriving home after a night out, while everyone was in bed, mum, dad, Agnes and Ted discovered the dog and the cockerel missing from their pens in the garden. On going into the house and putting on the light in the living room, they discovered the dog and the cockerel one each end of the settee fast asleep!!

For all that, our house was always full of laughter and music. As children, we would always sing ourselves to sleep. A good job we had no near neighbours. A few years later on we were able to have a piano in one room, and a small American organ in another. Dad would gather us all around, whilst he played one of the instruments. We would have to sing, one of us was always flat, and of course that someone was me. The others all had nice voices, and could play the piano, but unfortunately I must have been tone deaf. I couldn't do either! *Years later, I remarked about it to our local minister when we were discussing hymns and his remark cheered me up, he said, "The Lord didn't ask you to sing he just said to make a joyful noise. Great, that's just what I'll do."*

It was June 1934 and there were strikes still going on in London. Things hadn't improved much over the years. Olive's 15th birthday had arrived, and mum had bought her, a new white dress and new shoes. They had their friends around, and were playing records on the gramophone and having a lovely time in the garden. With all the noise that was going on, mum decided to investigate, and there was poor Olive crying her eyes out, feet first in the water barrel. Well you can imagine mum's reaction. The boyfriends soon had the smiles wiped from their faces, and they weren't allowed to forget it for a long time. But peace was restored once mum had got her inside and cleaned her up and changed her dress.

Agnes had got a new baby girl, Phyllis Constance. All of us children were playing outside when we saw the midwife arrive with her Gladstone bag, with *the 'baby inside," or so we were told"*. Phyllis's second name was Constance, after Agnes and Ted's landlady.

We also had our first visit from mums brother, our uncle Jack and his wife auntie Cissie. They were visiting London on some sort of business, and decided to come on a quick visit. Mum hadn't seen them for about ten years, we younger ones had never met them, but apparently he recognised us. Elsie remembers him stopping his car to ask, *'did we know where the Nicholls family lived?' After looking at us, he said to his wife, 'they belong to Amy', and then he spotted Jack coming down the road and as usual he'd been scrumping and had a load of apples stuffed up his shirt. Uncle Jack burst out laughing 'that's another one of our Amy's'.* Poor mum trying to make a good impression, but at least it broke the ice and made everyone laugh.

That year at Christmas, Jack had as usual in anticipation of what Father Christmas would be bringing him, placed a pillowcase, at the bottom of his bed. He was so very pleased, with what Father Christmas had left him the next morning, that he rushed downstairs, shouting; *"It's alright mum I've got the dinner"* and indeed he had. The pillowcase was full of vegetables, with a great big cabbage stuck right on the top. His elder sisters and the lodgers were teasing him, and told him to look in the cupboard, and there was his real Christmas present, a train set. I don't know what the rest of us had, but it must have been equally as good, as we were all treated the same. I also remember that at one time my brothers had a meccano set; we would have great fun building bridges and cranes. Another time I can remember they had a horse racing game. The game, consisted, of a piece of green canvas, which would stretch right across width of the table. At each end of the canvas, were steel clamps, which pulled the canvas tight. On each clamp was a handle, attached to the handle, was another piece of metal, which would then allow you to lift the four or five horses already set in the galloping position, up off the canvas. Then as you turned the handle, the horses would race along the table, the harder you turned, the faster the horses ran, shuddering all along, the length of the table. The screams that went on, with everyone shouting for their horse to win, it was great fun.

It was also the year that I was five years of age and started school. Not long after Uncle Jack's visit, mum came into a sum of money, where she received it from we younger one's can't remember. However, she managed to go on holiday back to Wales, for the first time in ten years. It wasn't long after her return home that the decision was made to move back to Wales. Well mum may have been going home, but we certainly weren't, and it was a little bit upsetting. Agnes came as well, enabling her and Ted, to go and visit his family in the Rhondda, and to show his two babies off to his mother. It was a very strange experience. Although they spoke English they also spoke Welsh, and it was very difficult to understand them. I went into the Infants, and we were being taught in both English and Welsh

Being taught Welsh was ok. Thinking back, it makes one wish that we had paid more attention, but we were all really homesick.

Winnie and Olive's boyfriends cycled up from where they lived in Benfleet, Essex to Cardiff for a weekend. One of them already had a bicycle; the other found a bike before it was lost. Both the girls made appointments to go to the hairdresser, to have their hair 'Marcel' waved. In between times they used to have a pair of curling tongs, which they placed either on the gas cooker or in the hot fire. Once the tongs were hot enough, they would then twirl them round by one handle to see how hot they were. They'd then, get some paper and if the paper singed, so would their hair. Once the tongs had cooled a wee bit, they would then curl their hair into waves. *"A fore runner of todays "hot brush".*

They would also use a little of *'Ponds Vanishing Cream'*, and face powder, and dab a little bit of perfume, *'Californian Poppy'*, or *'Evening in Paris'*, which came in a little blue bottle, with a silver top, but not too much in case dad told them off. Mum wouldn't go anywhere without a bit of powder on her face, although she'd preferred to use *'Velouty'*, a combination of foundation and powder. Once we even tried to make our own perfume with rose petals and water, but after a couple of weeks sitting going stagnant we had to throw it away.

Agnes and Ted lived in their own home opposite. Their house backed on to the railway, and there we would sit, on her high brick wall, and imagine the trains all going back home, wishing we were all on it as well. Saturday morning's mum's uncle Clem would come down and give us all our pocket money, sixpence each. That enabled us to go to the *'tuppenny rush'* children's show at the local cinema, plus a for *ha-penny* sweets. I can remember seeing *'Flash Gordon's Trip to Mars'*, and Charlie Chaplin, etc. Mum's cousin Ivor, would also call round on a Saturday morning. He would go up to the biscuit factory, which was located at the top of the street. He would then call in to see us on his way back home, with huge bags of broken biscuits. He would then ask mum if she wanted any, and off he went back to the factory get more bags for her, and Agnes. While he was gone Agnes, Winnie and Olive would sort through his bags looking for their favourite biscuit's. It was also at this time, we had a surprise visit from mum's brother Jack and his wife auntie Cissie. While we were at the front door, up rolled Uncle Jack in his open tourer car. It had two seats with a *'Dickie'* seat at the back. We all had a wonderful ride in his car, a couple of us sitting in his *'Dickie'* seat.

Elsie recalls, that one morning whilst having our breakfast of porridge before we all went to work and school, there was a knock on the front door. Dad answered it, and the next minute, he came back followed by two gypsy children, and their mother. He told us all to move up, and sat them down beside us at the table, and told mum to give them something to eat. When mum remonstrated with him about it, and said that they had six of their own children to feed. His reply was that *"we wouldn't miss one spoonful each from out of our bowls and that we had to share what we had."*

All this would go on for years, with dad bringing strange people in to share what little we had, although, to be honest, we never went hungry. He didn't leave it at that though; there would be times when we gave up our beds because some people wouldn't have anywhere to sleep. All this went on because of all the unemployment and people being homeless and looking for work. As we got older, it didn't happen so much, things had improved some what, plus we children were getting more grown up and weren't so easily shifted out of our beds!

It was the beginning of 1936 and at this moment in time, there would be 2,700.000 people still unemployed that did not include counting the thousand of people, who weren't registered

Whilst we were living in Wales, I caught the Measles, and was restricted to the bedroom. I didn't mind that, as I was being thoroughly spoilt, until one day, I had an unexpected visitor. Agnes' eldest daughter went missing, she was nearly three years old, she had crossed the road, opened the front door, which was never locked anyway, and then crawled up the stairs, and climbed up onto my bed. There they found her. Well, there was a bit of a panic, because of the Measles; Agnes had kept her children away from the house. She didn't want her babies to catch it. However, after her toddler had absconded, she brought her other baby over to join the toddler and me in the bed, so that we could all have the Measles together. So instead of being bored, suddenly I had two babies in my bed.

According to mum, when Agnes was about five she also would go off on long walks to the local zoo, where she said, she went for a "sit down and a rest." Whereas her eldest daughter was a little bit wiser and would take herself off to the local police station. *She later recalled; it must have been the fruitcake they gave her.* Anyway, they became so used to her, the police would go along and ask Ted to come and bail his daughter out.

The thing I remember about Wales was the smell of the lovely 'Fish & Chip shop'. It was cooked in dripping in those days, and smelt like heaven, especially if you were hungry. Outside Agnes's house, was a street light. Jack would sling a bit of rope around the crossbar, just underneath the main light, and we would all take turns in swinging around it. We would swing out into the street and back on to the pavement, it was great fun.

In the house where we lived in Wales, Winnie,

Olive, and Elsie all shared a bedroom. Elsie remembers them having a large poster of 'Joan Blondell' *(a famous American actress of the time),* pinned on the wall in their bedroom. At meal times, they would both tease Elsie. One would say to the other, *" don't you think our Elsie looks just like Joan Blondell, she has the same lovely colour blonde hair and the big blue eyes that the film star has".* That would send poor old Elsie off. She'd start to cry, and as the crying increased, so did the teasing, until mum told them to leave her alone. Then one of them would sit her on their lap and give her a cuddle. If any of we younger ones got upset, we always had plenty of laps to sit on, and be comforted.

We didn't stay in Wales too long, although mum may have felt homesick for Wales; there were more of us feeling homesick for England. Winnie and Olive missed their boyfriends, and I don't think Ted was doing so well with the job situation. Remember that the Welsh people were still leaving their homes in search of work. And so we came back to England....

Chapter Three

The Depression in The 1930's

Agnes at this time was expecting her third baby, her sister-in-law Lil, had recently married and was expecting her first child. They both managed to get houses next door to each other. They had very long gardens, and Ted was able to grow a lot of vegetables, which helped supplement his wages. Years later when he didn't have such a large garden to work in, he managed to have an allotment where he would spend many happy hours. One would think that he'd have enough of digging all week. We went to Southend and spent most of our lives, living around that area. Shortly after we arrived back, Winnie and her long-term boyfriend were married, and she moved into her own place. That left five of us still at home, although sadly, it wasn't to stay that way for too long. It was around this time that Ted was working in Southend. He was working on a very large cinema called the *'Astoria'*, which was later to become the *'Odeon Cinema'*.

Cinemas were very glamorous places at that time; most of them were very large and seated lots of people, in the larger ones they would even include a restaurant and a ballroom. In some of the cinemas, they would have a wonderful *'Wurlizter'* organ, which would be played during the intervals. Different coloured lights would shine on them, whilst the organist played. They were truly majestic looking instruments. In some cinemas you could even order trays of tea, to be brought around to your seats during these musical intervals. Really the cinemas were wonderful magical places.

Winnie and her husband Bernard, were expecting

their first child, they had gone to the pictures, where she was taken ill. Poor mum, nobody had telephones then, and when she heard the news, she walked from where we lived in Westcliff to Rochford Hospital. Having stayed most of the night with Winnie, she then had to walk back home again, and arrange for us younger one's to go over to stay with Agnes, and let her know what was happening. She hadn't been home an hour, when a policeman came and told her that Winnie had died. As briefly mentioned earlier, this was due to Eclampsia. Off we went to Agnes, while mum and Olive went back over to the hospital. When people died in those days, in was the custom to bring the body back home, where they rested, until the funeral. Such was the case for Winnie. The front room was cleared to make room for the coffin and stands. While Winnie was at home, mum stayed with her, sitting in a chair beside the coffin *(which also contained her stillborn baby),* possibly there was a candle, and I remember a vase of Lilies. In the morning before going to school, we would go into see mum with Winnie, in order for her to check that we were all clean and tidy for school. I recall climbing on to mum's lap, where mum would be stroking Winnie's hair, and wiping her mouth. Winnie was then later buried with her stillborn baby. Winnie was just nineteen years old, just a few days after her birthday. *Since then I can't stand the smell or sight of Lilies. Many years later I remember, on visiting Olive. She pulled an old suitcase from out of a cupboard, and upon opening it, removed a rather long brown coat with a fox fur collar. Then she asked me if I remembered it. When I asked her whom it belonged to she told me it was Winnie's. That made me think she must have been a very smart young lady, with the face powder and the perfume and the 'Marcel' waved hair (remember we are speaking of the mid thirties), and how close Winnie and Olive had been.*

Like Winnie, her husband Bernard was also young, and he just couldn't handle the grief. So it was left to mum, to arrange her own daughter's funeral. Mum said that he wasn't even at the funeral, and they never saw or heard of him again. Even his best friend Jim, who was Olives' boyfriend, and who she was to marry a few months later had not heard from him. Mum wasn't too pleased about the forthcoming marriage, she felt that at sixteen Olive was too young, and it was too soon after loosing Winnie. Maybe she felt she was losing Olive as well.

It wasn't all sadness. Agnes had her third child and only son David James. Her sister-in-law Lil had a little girl, Nora. The next baby was Olives and Jim's, a daughter Pamela. Olives' husband Jim had a precarious job working on a farm. When the farmer didn't need you any more you would be sacked and have to vacate your house which would be tied to the job. I can well remember looking out of the window and seeing them roll up in an open top lorry, which the farmer had lent them together with a driver, to help them remove their belongings; Olive sitting in the front seat clutching her baby, who was still wrapped up in a shawl in her arms. *(Jim was unable to drive until many years later).*

The Agriculture workers were very badly treated. Indeed it had only been in 1872, that the National Agriculture Union had been founded. Just about sixty years previously to Jim being employed as one of the farm workers. Things had improved a little but not really so much as to make a lot of difference. They still had to work very hard from sun-up to sundown for a pittance.

Agnes' eldest daughter, often stayed over, and when we

were getting ready for school she would want to go as well. So, as not to upset her, mum would get her ready, and give her *'ha-penny'* for her milk and Elsie would have to take her to school. Off, she would go, as pleased as punch, to sit beside Elsie all morning. She would have her bottle of milk. At playtime, she would also be out in the playground with the big girls. It was allowed, in certain circumstances for an older child in a family to take a younger brother or sister to school with them. She would only been about four years old at the time. When we arrived home for our dinner she would sit on her nan's lap and tell her all about her day at school, then still sitting on her nan's lap she would promptly fall asleep, worn out with all the days events. Mum's grandchildren later on in their lives would say, that sitting on Nan's lap was like sitting in a big warm cosy armchair.

It was during this summer, that dad had a job back on the water, but only on the pleasure boats. They would pick up passengers from Tower Hill in London and sail down the river to Southend Pier, where they would pick up more passengers, and off they would go for a day trip to Margate or Ramsgate. One day to our delight mum told us to get ready. We were all going to meet dad and go on his boat for a trip to Margate, it was called The *'Queen of Thanet'*. Dad met us on the end of the pier and took us down to the saloon bar, and there he introduced us to the captain. He said to dad "*Are these your daughter's? Dad said "yes", we've had five daughter's altogether", "Oh, he said, I've got loads of boys. I'll swap you one of your girls for one of my boys."* So Dad pointing at me said, "*Oh, you can have her*!"

We had a lovely day out and even Jack behaved himself, he was too fascinated being at sea and going down to the engine room, listening to the sounds, and watching the movement of the engines to get up to any pranks.

Whenever Olive arrived home mum would have to move our beds around to enable Olive and Jim to have a room to themselves with all their bits around them. We became used to it, for it wasn't unusual for dad to bring people home for the night and to give them a meal and a bed. There were still lots of homeless people around searching for work and somewhere to live, Trust dad to find them, we didn't have much ourselves but what we did have, we had to share.

When we were young, we didn't have any of these worries, like dad said, *'you will have enough worries when you get older so enjoy your childhood',* which we did. That didn't mean that we didn't have any jobs to do. Len would go around the shops asking for spare boxes, and then he would chop them up for firewood. With a couple of the larger decent boxes, he and Jack made a barrow, with a large box fixed on old pram wheels. They would go around knocking on peoples' doors, to sell it at sixpence a bucket or a penny a bundle. Len also had a job delivering medicines for the doctors. In those days the doctors would dispense their own medicines and after school the boys would deliver them to the patients, some of the boys were only about twelve but, as long as they could handle and ride their bikes the job was theirs. They rode special bikes with a large basket attached to the front. On either side of the basket frame, were two metal supports, which enabled the bicycle to remain upright when the boys got off. Then off they would go, hail, rain, or shine. All these jobs were after school.

Elsie also had a little job, helping in the corner greengrocers, the owner's son had a crush on her, and we used to tease her to ask him if we could go into the backyard, of the shop, to look for *'specky'* apples and oranges. She would be most indignant, but off she would go with her gym slip half way up her thighs, and then beckon us into his back yard with the instruction especially to Jack, only take the rotten ones. It was like a kid's heaven, rummaging around in there.

Elsie at this time wanted to go 'tap dancing 'classes, but unfortunately mum couldn't afford the money. Employment wise things weren't much better. Mum had got herself a job, as a cook in a restaurant down by the *'Kursaal',* leaving Elsie to look after Jack and myself. But Elsie wasn't going to be denied her moment of stardom, she would sneak into the dancing class and the teacher would allow her to watch. Once she even allowed her to take part in the tap dancing class. She then decided that she would put on her own show, with me being a willing accomplice. When she had enough of an audience, she would charge them a *'ha-penny'* each, to watch her and me perform. They would have to sit on the back steps, and Elsie and I would then prance out of the coal shed, which was our make believe dressing room, and it was conveniently placed at the bottom of the stairs, and there we strutted our stuff!

'Shirley Temple' was a very famous child star then, and every little girl would try to imagine that she was just another Shirley Temple. Another, of the child stars was 'Jane Withers', and of course there was still 'Ginger Rogers' and 'Fred Astaire', all of them famous movie stars. These are just who my sister and I would pretend to be. Trying to dance and sing to *"On the good ship lollipop", "I'm putting on my top hat"* etc. By the time we had got through the first one, the kids were demanding their money back, where upon, she would box their ears and make them stay. Couldn't blame them really, Elsie may have been ok, as she had been to a few lessons, but it didn't help having me as accomplice, I could neither sing nor dance. In the end everyone got fed up.

Alas, our moment of stardom had come and gone, however for their *'ha-penny'*, Elsie had provided them with refreshments of home-made lemonade, (made with the crystal's), and broken biscuits. Mum had also bought her a pair of second hand ballet shoes to make up for her disappointment in being unable to go to tap dancing lessons.

It wasn't all doom and gloom. We used to have lovely times, playing in the streets with the neighbours' kids. We would have tops and whips. The whips would be wrapped around the spindle and the tops we would then colour with crayons or coloured paper, then kneel on the top and pull the whip, to see how far the top would go spinning away with all the pretty colours shinning on the top. There would be marbles to run down the gutter, to see who could win the most marbles, by hitting the one in front. The girls would have skipping ropes stretched across the road, and we would take turns to skip through it or when we got fed up with that we would jump over it and see who could jump the highest. We would also play *'hopscotch'*, *'leap-frog'*, and acrobats up the brick walls. Careful, to tuck our dresses into our knicker-legs. We always seemed to find lots to do, and have lots of energy to do it all in. There would always be someone keeping an eye on the children, if only behind net curtains. Most peoples' front doors would be on the latch, and if it was locked the key would be hanging on a piece string through the letterbox. So we where never locked out.

In the summer time we would spend a lot of days on the beach, with jam sandwiches and a bottle of lemonade. We made the lemonade ourselves by buying lemonade powder from the sweet shop. Whoever went for it would have their fingers inspected, in case they had been dipping into it on the way home. The wise ones dipped their tongue instead. We spent the whole day on the beach, if we got thirsty we were able, to get water from the drinking fountains. They had a little metal cup attached by a chain, or you could place your mouth straight over the fountain. These fountains were situated all along the seafront. I don't believe they have them any more. If we were lucky enough to find a couple of lemonade bottles, we could take them back to the shop, and exchange them for money. Hopefully, enough to buy a *'Rossi'* ice cream, or an *'Eldrado'* but they were much smaller than the *'Rossi'*.

We would also try to find, as many, beer bottles as we could, as well as the pop bottles. We would then, take them back to the Off Licence, and hopefully get enough pennies to buy some sweets. We could buy loads of sweets for a few pence, but if we didn't make enough money to share, then we would buy *'gob stoppers'*. They were large sweets, which, would just about fit into your mouth. We would take it in turns, having a suck until the colour changed then it would be popped into someone else's mouth. Watching each other very carefully, that the colour didn't change twice. If it did, you had to miss a go, or you could buy liquorice laces, put one end into each other's mouth to see who got to the middle first. The boys would play football, or knock down ginger, and then all the kids would scarper. As *'Guy Fawkes Day'* approached, we would take a Guy out and collect pennies to buy fire works, then at Christmas time we would go carol singing. There were loads more games we played.

But the best game of all was when we couldn't go out. It was mums' bed that we used as a trampoline. Mums' bed was one of those beds, with an old-fashioned iron frame, with all the bits of brass on each end. It had this big box spring mattress on it, and every week, on bed changing day she would go around it with a long handled box spanner and tighten all the nuts on the spring mattress. She would then scrub into each corner with a scrubbing brush, on top of that went a thick mattress and then a feather one, fresh linen and lovely plumped up bolster and pillows. It didn't stay like that for long. It was like a magnet to us kids. We would creep up the stairs and go into her bedroom and climb onto the bed. It was so high that we would need help, to climb onto it, and then we would see who could jump the highest, and touch the ceiling. Sometimes, there would be four of us jumping on it with a couple more waiting their turn. At one time being over enthusiastic the bed came off the iron frame, and slipped sideways, so did we kids, and it came to rest on the wall opposite, with us lot underneath the bedclothes and the two mattresses'. One can imagine the pandemonium that caused. It was a long time before we were once again allowed to venture into the bedroom to have another jump on the bed.

There is an expression today; did you feel the earth move? Well whoever is living in our old house when they walk down the garden they will surely be speaking the truth. Because that's where mum's old bedspring is buried, beside the old coal shed!!

The next escapade was when Jack discovered that by pulling the chain in the outside toilet and lifting up the manhole cover, we could see everything that went by. So Jack decided to make some ships out of newspaper, and one of us would take it in turns to put the ships down the toilet, then pull the chain, dash out into the garden, then we could watch the so called ships sail by. We were having great fun until mum, who happened to be in the kitchen, doing a bit of washing, spotted us. She shouted to us to stop and put the cover back on to the manhole before anyone had an accident. Well she must have had a premonition. We put the manhole cover back on *(or so we thought)!*

The next thing is mum comes sailing out of the back door, with a bundle of washing in her arms, when she disappeared, straight down the manhole. Mother being no lightweight, we couldn't get her out, when we got too close to her she was trying to clip our ears, and saying *"you wait till I get hold of you two you little flamers,"* which was one of Mums favourite expressions. In the end we had to get help from the neighbours to pull her out. We both hopped it pretty quick. After a good telling off we had to go to our rooms, and stay there without any tea. When the rest of the family came home, we could hear roars of laughter, and mum saying, *"its nothing to laugh about"*, and then laughing herself. We did have our tea after all, she brought us up some bread and jam and a cup of tea, but we had to stay in our rooms, which was very painful. They certainly gave Jack the right name William; he was just like the boy in the Racheal Cromptons *"Just William"* books.

Good job she never saw us up the trees down by the brook! Jack would give me *tuppence ha-penny*, to go into the tobacconist, to ask for five woodbines for my dad, and a little book of matches please. The man would say, *"are you sure these are for your dad?"* Then he'd give me the cigarettes, we would sit up in the branches of the trees, coughing and feeling sick, but we persevered. After the *'ciggys'* if he didn't have any more money, he tried rolling cabbage leaves in bits of newspaper, but that really made us sick, so he gave the smoking up for a while

Dad was very strict in regards to us all doing as we were to told and not to answer back was fatal, but he never ever raised his hand to any of us. Mum was the disciplinarian, handing out the discipline via her shoe or slipper but as I have said before, she always missed, but it always made us duck to see this object flying through the air. Dad was also very strict with us, as regards our table manners. At meal times, we weren't allowed at the table, unless we had washed and our faces and hands and tidied our hair. Jack's neck was then investigated for tide marks. If your elbows were happening to be resting on the table, along would come the blade of his knife or dessert spoon, whichever happened to be in his hand at the time, and knock our elbows off the table. He then would ask if you were tired, if so then go to bed, otherwise sit up straight

We were also never allowed to reach across the table and help ourselves. We had to wait until the food was passed to you. Although our dinners were placed before us, we still had to wait till mum sat down. I suppose with so many sitting down at meal times they had to have some sort or order, otherwise we may have been like a rugby scrum. Mum and dad were brought up with Victorian values and these same values they tried to install in their children. When we had finished eating our knives and forks would have to be placed directly in front of us on the plate. If they weren't, he would ask if you had finished, if so, then place your cutlery so that other people would know that you had done so.

It was about this time that Elsie sat her school exams; she was very intelligent and clever. She passed her exams and won a place at *St Bernards' Convent*. Although her fees, would have been paid for, by the education authority. It still wouldn't have paid for her winter and summer uniforms that she needed, plus the sports equipment. Unfortunately that was something else that poor old Elsie would be unable to have, a good education. She recently told me, that after that episode mum went to an auction and bought her a piano for one pound to try and make up for her disappointment, in being unable to go to St Bernards. Jack started to have music lessons, and did very well. Years' later Agnes daughter eldest daughter would do the same and won several certificates.

When Len was about fourteen years of age he got a job, as a *'dingy boy'* at the *'Westcliff Yacht Club'*. Jack or Elsie would have to take his dinner down to him. The dinner would be placed in-between two dinner plates, with a tea towel wrapped around it, and then placed in your hands, with the strict instructions, *"don't upset the gravy"!* On one occasion Elsie and Jack were now-where to be found. There was only me, and at that time, I was seven years old, but I still remember it clearly. Those dinner plates were placed in my hands, with the same instructions *"don't upset the gravy!"* and off I went. It was about a three mile walk or even longer, across two main roads then down a flight of steps to the seafront. You would then have to walk along the esplanade until you saw the ship moored, out on the river. All the way on my errand, going through my head was *"don't upset the gravy"!!* On approaching the ship, placed on the esplanade opposite the ship, was a big ships bell which you rang, then Len appeared on the gangplank, jumped into the dingy and sculled over to the esplanade to pick up members of the Yacht club. But this time it was only me, with his dinner, still clasped in my hands, terrified that I had upset the gravy!! Len said *it was all right*, and he would take me aboard the ship. So off I went into the dinghy, and I was rowed out to the ship by my big brother. Arriving on board, he took me down to the galley, where I was given a glass of lemonade and a big arrowroot biscuit. So, the errand didn't seem so bad after that. No wonder Jack and Elsie didn't mind going, if at the end of their errand, they got lemonade and a biscuit. It was also that year that Len brought me a birthday present. It was my eighth birthday, and he had bought me a little celluloid doll sitting in her little bath, with a bath tray across the bath, and a long handled brush, all made out of celluloid.

Mum worked very long hours at the restaurant, she would leave very early in the morning to catch the buses so as to get to work on time. She would then arrive back home long after, we had been put to bed, by Elsie. But she still made time to wash our clothes and make sure we were all clean, before she herself went to bed. I can still recall her coming in to the bedrooms, to make sure we were all right, and picking up our clothes, which we had worn that day, and leaving fresh ones out for the morning. We didn't have so many clothes that she could afford to leave them dirty. I can still hear her saying *"Have you changed your under wear? If you have an accident and end up in hospital I don't want to be told my kids were dirty"*. In the end we would reply; *"Its ok Mum, we'll make sure we change our underwear before we have the accident!"*

This was the year that they celebrated their Silver Wedding. They had cards from their relation's, including one from grandma in Penzance, and a couple from dad's cousins. Their ex lodgers had brought them a tea service which unfortunately has all gone, although we still see the same pattern in old films. They most probably had a Saffron cake from grandma as well as her card. Every year on dad's birthday, she would send him a Saffron cake, with a letter enclosed. Having a parcel delivered to the house was quite a novelty; we would stand there gazing at this brown-papered object all neatly tied up with string, waiting for dad to arrive home. To make matters worse when he did eventually arrive, he would neatly untie the knots in the string, roll the string around his fingers, and then start unwrapping the paper; once that was done he would then open the box, lift out this yellow fruit cake and place it on a plate. Then he would say *"right Amy, save me a couple of slices and give the rest to the children"*. Well poor grandma's cake didn't last five minutes after that, it was real *"ansome"* with a bit of butter on it. Even during the war years when she was able, she never forgot to send her boy Willie his Saffron cake

Leonard after his summer job had finished, like his father before him, decided to join the Merchant Navy. Also like his father, he was ill equipped for the voyage, but off he sailed to Nova Scotia in Canada. During the winter months, being in Nova Scotia, you might just as well have been in the Arctic, I don't recall too much about that time, only that he came home with a big canvas bag slung over his shoulder, and smelling of the sea, and he was wearing a blue and white woollen hat, plus, like his father he brought home a stray in the shape of another young boy. Because he was a Scot everyone on board ship called him *'Jock'*, so we did the same. That was about the only time mum had her garden turned over, he would spend hours planting vegetables, what his real name was I don't know but to us he was just *Jock*.

If ever mum had suggested to dad that it was about time he did something with the garden, he would answer her, *"yes m'dearr"*, and have a walk around the garden smoking either his pipe or a cigarette, as if the garden was some big estate. Then he would come in, put his jacket on and call out *"won't be long m'dearr"*, and that would be the last she'd see of him, until the feeling that he ought to do something with the garden had passed away. Maybe he went off to the snooker hall, according to Len dad was a very good snooker player, and won several silver cups. Maybe when he was short of money, he would go to the local snooker hall and play for money. Maybe the silver cups are still languishing in a pawnshop some where. Well I'm sure that dad would rather have his children fed, than have silver cups displayed on his mantle.

In these impoverished times, people used the pawnshops regularly. One of our neighbours happened to be in our house one day, when his daughter came in, and asked her father if she could have the pawn ticket for her ring. From his inside pocket, where most men keep their wallets, he pulled out a sheaf of them, just like a pack of playing cards. Mum reckoned he had the whole streets supply. On Monday mornings, it was mostly the women, who would line up outside the pawnshop or *"Uncles"* as he was called, with bundles of bedding tucked under their arms. Usually, it was a bit of jewellery such as their wedding rings, or their husband's pocket watch, or even their husband's best suit, which was usually the only one they had, and it would have to be recovered from the pawnbrokers, before the following weekend.

Those were the days too, when, if we children spied a certain person walking down the street carrying a large bag, we would rush in shouting, *"mum, the gas man is here"*, *"thank the lord for that"*, she would say, *"Now we can get some groceries in"*. At that time, all the gas used in the house was for cooking and heating the water, especially in the summer, when the fire wasn't lit, for then we usually lit the Ascot water heater for bathing. Some people were still using gas for lighting and gas fires, so periodically the Gas Company would have to empty the meters and send the collector round all the houses in the street. Hence, the great excitement when he was spotted. As soon as he knocked on the front door, mum would usher him in to the back living room as though he was royalty. Then quickly make sure the table was cleared, so that no pennies went astray. Then, with strict instruction to watch that he didn't put any in his pocket. It was quite fascinating to watch him. First of all, he would clamber about in the gas cupboard, and bring out the deep metal tray, that contained all the pennies, which he would the empty onto the table. The money would all flow across the table, with us watching that none fell on the floor; his fingers would go like lightning, counting the money; then placing it, in neat piles on the table; placing the piles of pennies into little blue bags. One or two, always seemed to disappear into his coat pocket. Then, out would come his book to check how much gas you had used against what he had taken from the meter. He would call out, *"I've finished, if you would like to come and check your rebate, and sign for it".* , In mum would come, usually wiping her hands on a towel, as if she had been very busy in the kitchen, (with her ears cocked all the while, the money was tingling). Check her rebate, and thank him very much, just as though he was personally giving her the money. After he had gone, she would then make a list of the essentials she had run out off, and it was usually Elsie who had to go to the shops. We'd then all have a penny to spend for some sweets, hopefully ones that lasted a long time. What was left would have to see her through the week.

Agnes, by this time had another baby girl, Irene, it was 1938. It was also about this time, that Agnes, walked, from where they lived in Hadleigh, to borrow some money from mum at her place of work. She did this twice, I can remember mum saying, "how angry she was with her, for walking all that way". It certainly was a long way, but people in those days didn't think anything of walking long distances. Mum said, she should have written a letter, which, would only cost about a penny, and mum would have received it the next day. Elsie would then have gone over on the bus to give her some money. As I have said Ted was in work and he certainly wasn't lazy, but unfortunately they didn't get paid if it rained. He may well have been to work all week, but come pay day he would arrive home with maybe only a couple of days pay, all the men working in construction in those days were treated the same, whether they be Carpenters, Bricklayers, or what have you. None of them got paid, if they were rained off.

But Agnes and Ted's luck was about to change a little, in modern day language he was 'Head Hunted'. A construction firm had the contract to lay drains and sewerage pipes for a new estate that was in the process of being built by the 'Bell Pub' in Southend. They were having problems shoring up the sides of the deep ditches that were necessary, before they could lay the new drains and sewerage pipes. It would appear, that the earth around that area was very sandy, and the sides of the ditches as they were being dug out, kept collapsing. This job was very important for the safety of the men, who were working there digging out these deep ditches. It was time and money, so they needed a good timber man and Ted was that man. They offered him more money than he was receiving at his present place of work, plus if it rained, instead of getting no pay he would get half pay, he would also be in charge of the men working with him. In those days, the wages worked out at a shilling per hour. Apparently, at one time there was a strike, the men demanded more money for working standing in water. They then, allowed the men an extra penny for having to work in the water. Lucky for those ones who had Wellington Boots, if they hadn't any, they would have to work in their boots all day, and trust to luck to get them dry before they started work the next morning. No wonder Ted liked taking mums home- made, cough mixture to work, he said it kept him warm.

Well Ted couldn't refuse that offer, but he would have to cycle all the way from Hadleigh, along the Arterial road, along Princes Avenue to the Rochford road, to where the Bell Pub now stands. Len still remembers going to watch the men working and to see Ted, it was quite a popular occupation for most men, leaning over the barriers to watch the other men at work.

At that time, they didn't have mechanical diggers and such like; everything had to be done by hand even the removal of the earth that would be building up each side of the ditches. All the earth would have to be shovelled up and placed into wheelbarrows. The wheel barrows would then be pushed over to waiting Lorries, the men would then have to run up the ramps, pushing these heavy wheel barrows, to deposit the earth on the floor of the Lorries, and then the Lorries were driven away.

Of course, all these dangerous ditches and heaps of earth couldn't be left unguarded over night. The company had to employ a night watch man. It was his job, to make sure that all the lamps were working, that the wicks in the lamps were trimmed, and that they had sufficient paraffin to take them through the night. He would then have to sit in a little hut, with just enough room for him to be able to sit down. Woe be tied him, if he happened to be a very tall person, unfortunately his feet would stick out of the opening. Periodically through the night he would have to walk around the site, to make sure all the lamps were still alight. Placed just outside the opening, he would have his brazier, on which he was able to heat his tea, and any soup or meal that he had taken to work. It was quite a creepy job, especially if it was a foggy night when you couldn't see a hand in front of you, let alone a night light. Even sound was muted on foggy nights.

Unfortunately things weren't so lucky for Jim and Olive; he was laid off from his job, therefore having to leave their tied cottage. She was back home once again with her little girl Pamela and her new baby Patricia, so there were two new babies in the family. Dad was away so Mum had room for them. Dad had got a job opening restaurants for a departmental store very similar to the" British Home Stores". In this job he was travelling all over the country, organising the setting up and the opening up, of their restaurants. It was called 'Hills & Steels'. In fact they opened one just under the Railway Bridge in Southend high street. The same type of stores as 'Timothy Whites' and 'Taylors'

Jim however managed to get a job as a salesman for the 'Fuller Brush' firm. He would have to ride his bike to a certain area allocated to him, and try and sell as many Fuller Brush products as he could. All the Items that they sold were displayed in a large brown leather case, which of course he'd had to pay for together with the contents. Jim was doing fine, until one day he had all his sample goods stolen, and having no money to replace all the items, that job was finished. His next job was with 'Walls' Ice Cream, going around on one of their special bikes. They had refrigerated boxes in the front, and would ring a cycle bell to attract peoples' attention especially the children's. Around all the sides of the bike, was written *" Stop Me and Buy One"*, they would sell little rounds of ice cream covered up in a paper wrapper (the same size as sample paint pots that one can buy today). You would then place it into a cornet, or they would give you two wafer biscuits instead of the cornet. They would also sell all different flavoured ice, lollies, (fruit flavoured coloured water), which were triangular in shape and they were covered in a car-board wrapper. They would do a good trade, especially in the summer months. However when the summer ended he finally went back to the work he loved best, and they moved back to the country.

It wasn't only this country that had all the unemployment problems. There was a worldwide recession at this time, with the exception of course in Germany where they were already building up large stocks of armaments.

Years later, a friend of mine would relate, how when his Father and Mother took all of their family from Hungary to Canada. There wasn't any work to be had, and of course no social help at all in those days, the only help they got was from the churches, he and his father would go around looking in the dustbins behind hotels, restaurants, and supermarkets. Any bits and pieces they found his mother would make some sort of meal, even chicken heads and fish heads. It would make you feel ill just to listen to his stories about how rough times had been.

It was 1938, unknown to us children, the world was about to enter a very black period in all of our lives, and when it was all over, our childhood would have finished and thousands of the children who were alive today wouldn't be here. Indeed the horror had already started for some children in Europe. But in the meantime for us, life was good, it was summer, and we were young.

During the summer months when we were off school, we not only went on to the beach to enjoy our selves, we also went to the park and played rounders and cricket. We also went to the brook, with a jam jar and a long handled net to catch 'tiddlers'. If we heard of any of the Sunday school's that were having an outing, we would join up at the school and go on the outings as well. I can remember once, Jack and I went up to London on such an outing. We went to the London Zoo on the train, and then on the underground, by which time my egg sandwiches were coming out of the wrapping paper. I started to get upset, and told Jack that I was going to lose them, so Jack suggested that we had better eat them then. So there was my dear brother Jack helping to scoff my sandwiches on the train. However when we finally arrived at the zoo, I made sure he shared what remained of his sandwiches with me. To me, my brother Jack was just a stomach on legs, especially at meal times. If dad wasn't around, and we had tapioca pudding, after he had finished his pudding he would lean right over mine and call my pudding all sorts of horrible names e.g. 'snot & bogey pudding'. As brothers are known to do, hoping that I would leave it, but I was quite wise to his tricks, and knowing him so well I would completely ignore him, much to his disappointment. Mum would tell him he could go and scrape the dish that the pudding was made in; we had to take it in turns to do that.

Going to the Sunday schools was great. We were able to join in lots of things, such as, sausage and mash nights. We would have to take our own plates and a cup, then we would also have a cup of cocoa, sometimes we would have magic lantern shows. Elsie remembers going to one church where we were all given a card, and on it was written, *"B Y O G "*, when she asked Mum what it meant she told her it said *"Bring Your Own Grub",* we didn't think too much off that to say the least.

Elsie also belonged to the Girl Guide's. I belonged to the Brownies and the boys were in the Scouts. We had great fun sitting around pretend campfires, and singing campfire songs. They also taught us a bit, about First Aid, how to light a fire, and make all sorts of knots, and loads of other things.

We would also go to the cinema, on Saturday mornings. Just as we did when we lived in Cardiff, our favourite one though was the Gaumont in Southend, it was once an old theatre and it had three floors to it we kids would go way up in the gods which cost only tuppence. To get in, the boys would then start to throw stink bombs down onto the people sitting way down below in the stalls, when the boys ran out of stink bombs; they would start using their pea shooters. The ammunition would be dried peas. If we went to the 'Mascot' or the 'Strand', you couldn't use that sort of ammunition the usherettes would come along and grab the boys by the scruff of their jackets and turf them out. If, like Jack, they had one of their sisters with them, *(girls weren't expected to use peashooters and other nasty things).* Before being dragged out, he would say go down to the toilets behind the curtain, and don't let any one see you, and open the fire exit door, so that he could bunk back in. Of course if we only had enough money just for one ticket, he would leave me outside a fire exit door, then he would pay for his ticket and then drag me in through the fire door

Sometimes Jack's pockets in his jacket or trousers would look rather heavy, and mum would make him turn them out, telling him off about breaking his pockets down with all the weight of the bits and pieces he would have tucked away. Out would come; bits of lengths of string, a couple of marbles, a bit of rag, he used as a hankie and other obnoxious things. A few old peas' left over from his ammunition, maybe his pea-shooter or his catapult, whichever weapon the boys were using that week, plus lots of fluff. We waited with much trepidation, to see if at the end, after getting down to the fluff, and before mum would see us we would come across a half-eaten toffee or a boiled sweet. If it was all covered in fluff, we would rinse it off under the tap (or if there wasn't a tap available he would suck the muck off) and we would share it. I can hear mum saying *"you pair of dirty little flamers"!* Good job she never saw us suck the fluff of or we would definitely have had our ears boxed.

On a Saturday mum and Elsie would go shopping into Southend on a tram. They were very noisy things, and you would have to take care in alighting from them. The tramlines run in the middle of the street. The overhead rails sometimes sparked with electricity, more so when they approached a junction. They would later do away with the trams and convert to the trolley bus, which were wonderfully smooth running and quiet.

On arriving in Southend, one of the first ports of call would be the Victoria Arcade, which was better known as the Talza Arcade. In we would go, heading straight for 'Wells', a large open fronted store. It sold bacon, and different cheeses, all sorts of cooked meats and loads of other things. All of these, goods, were displayed in full array in front of the counter, for the customers to see. The only thing was that you would have to lean over the top of them, to be able to point out to the assistant, what you wanted. But, the first line, of goods for you to see, and set directly in the front, was these glass-topped tins of biscuits. We would peer down into these tins trying to imagine what delights they held. There would be those 'Garibaldi' biscuits which some people called 'Squashed Fly' biscuits, plus, little iced ones, and many more. Behind the tins, built up into a huge display were all the broken ones. You could buy big bags of these, very similar to those we had brought in Cardiff. Most of the people would buy these, with the remark, *"well you have to break them before you can eat them."* They also sold packets of dried peas and dried butter beans, which also contained a little tablet of bi-carbonate of soda. Mum would put these to soak overnight in basins with a plate on the top, already for our Sunday dinner. Can you imagine today using all that bi-carb?!

During the war, there were loads of posters around telling you what to save, one of which was asking you to save fuel for munitions. Well on a Sunday after dinner, (with all that bicarbonate of soda, which caused a lot of wind), I bet there was loads of gas floating around the streets it's a pity the government didn't come up with an idea on how bottle and to save it!

On leaving 'Wells', you continued on through the arcade towards the smell and the noise of the animals in the pet shop. You could hear the screeching of the birds, the cries of the puppies and kittens; they would also have a couple of monkeys in there with a chain around their necks.

When you think about it, today it must have been a like a chamber of horrors for those poor creatures.

On leaving the pet shop, you would come across a more pleasant scene, the world of books, 'Bobbins' Bookshop. As well as selling new books, they also sold second hand ones, plus magazines and comics. We were all encouraged to read books at home, if mum saw you standing around looking bored she would ask if you had anything to do. If the answer was no, her reply would always be *"well find yourself a book to read"*!

Also in the arcade would be this wonderful toy shop, the front window was completely fitted out with model train sets, "chew", "chew", "chewing" their way, through the make believe Alps, complete with snow. Up and down the mountains, through English villages, these little trains would wend their merry way. As well as the children being fascinated by the trains, so would the men.

Still walking on there would be a china shop, with

the china stacked so high, that it looked as though it would topple over any minute; maybe the shop keeper as you passed by hoped it would, and then be able to charge you for breakage.

All these shops were in the arcade, plus many more, it was a good place to be especially if it was raining. Coming out the other side, facing you would be one of our favourite cinema's the 'Gaumont', where Jack and I had probably already been that morning to the tuppenny rush, and so the shopping continued. Off mum would go, down the high street, peering into windows to see things to buy that she couldn't afford. If she had happened to have gone into 'Sopers', the drapery store they would have seats beside the counter for the customers to sit down whilst making their purchases, You would see all these little metal cups racing along the ceiling. The sales assistant, would place your bill and your money into the metal cups, then she would pull a handle, hanging down its side, and away it would go, straight into the cashiers little office which was raised so that cashier could see the whole of the store. Within seconds, back it would come, with your change and the bill. Maybe that is something they could adopt today, perhaps there wouldn't then be so many robberies at the checkouts. It is no wonder someone always went with her, she would arrive home heavy laden with loads of shopping, smiling all over her face, especially if she happened to get an aitchbone of beef that would have to be put into two bags. After unpacking the shopping she would then make a cup of tea and we would all have a cup and sort out our favourite biscuits from all the broken ones. One day, I mentioned to mum, that the lady next door had a wooden barrel on her sideboard with silver handles, where she kept her biscuits and why didn't we have one. Well you can guess what her answer was; *"the biscuits don't last long enough in this house to have much use made of it".*

This aitchbone of beef, was in fact the rump bone of the animal, (the main reason for it being so cheap), however the butchers always left plenty of meat on it. After having her tea off mum would go back into the kitchen, where she would start to brandish her carving knife, (of course after sharpen it on the back door step), and get to work boning this beef. Out of it she would get a large roasting joint, for our Sunday dinner, loads of meat for in the week plus the beef bone for stew. So you see it was quite a thrifty buy with so many mouths to feed.

Mum would keep all her old cups without their handles, so that when she made our meat puddings in the week we would all have our own individual ones. Also I can remember her at teatime, if we happened to be having bread and golden syrup she would drip our initials on the bread, and then we would spread the syrup ourselves.

Also on a Saturday, either Len and Elsie, or Elsie and Jack would have to go to the local bakery, and join the queue waiting for the delivery vans coming back from their rounds, with the bread and cakes that the deliverymen had been unable to sell. They would then sell it all of at half price. It made lovely bread pudding in the week.

On a Sunday, if the ice cream man came around we would go out with a basin and buy some. It was lovely having a spoonful of that, in a glass of ice-cream soda. We would also have 'Tizer' or a 'shandy', all of that, with the lovely smell of the roast dinner cooking in the oven. As we got older and dad wasn't around we would all have a bit of the Sunday paper to read whilst we waited for our dinner. Sunday teatime, we would always have some jelly and blancmange dad's favourite for tea. Mum would make it in basins and put it to set outside on the windowsills, with plates to on the top to protect it. You always knew who was having jelly and blancmange that day; all the neighbours' windowsills had basins on them. If the weather was a bit warm, we would sometimes have salad, which really only consisted of a lettuce leaf, tomato, cucumber, spring onions, sticks of celery placed in a jug, home made cake and bread and butter. If we didn't have the jelly and blancmange we would have a tin of fruit and evaporate milk, if the fruit happened to be pineapple chunks, when you poured the milk on it would appear as though the whole thing had curdled. Of course we only had all that when mum was bit flushed.

On the Sunday evening, we would all have to get ready to go to the chapel were dad was the organist and choirmaster. It was quite a long bus ride away, and we would like to sit on the top of the bus, sucking a few sweets. We were allowed to do so as mum and dad were busy sucking 'nippits' themselves to take away the smell of their cigarette smoke and the pint of beer that they'd had at dinnertime

On coming home from the chapel on the Sunday evening, we would then have supper; usually it would be sandwich and a cup of cocoa. In those days they would put a little farm animal on the top of the cocoa tin which we would collect. Although Elsie being a member of the 'Ovaltine's Club', preferred that. Mum would then start to fill the copper with water, and make sure the little fire underneath was all ready to light the following morning, in order to start the weekly washing. Next in would go the 'Oxydol' or 'Rinso' and then all her white washing to soak overnight. Washing day was a very busy day. All the whites had to be boiled and poked down every so often. Coloured things and woollens were washed by hand in the kitchen sink.

The rinsing of all the washing was also done in the kitchen sink. The big round copper stick would then be rolled around a sheet and the sheet would then be lifted out of the copper and placed into the sink for rinsing. It would then all be twisted around mums arms, and then she would place it into a small tin bath. Once the rinsing had finished. It would then have to be rung out; this was usually done in the back garden. The big mangles with their heavy wooden rollers were too large to be placed in a small kitchen; hopefully if it wasn't raining the washing would then be pegged on the line to dry. Very often there would be a bit of a race amongst the neighbours as to which one had their washing on the line first.

These proceedings went on for most of the day, and when we came home from school at lunchtime even the tablecloths would be in the wash. The table would be laid with the Sunday newspaper, our knives and forks neatly in place, Mondays dinner was always the same, cold meat and pickle with 'bubble and squeak'. If there were any pudding or pie left over from the day before, we would have that as well. If anyone asked if there was any 'afters', back would come the reply *"Thank yourselves lucky you've had your befores'!* Mum, had a couple of black horsehair dinning room chairs. The little covers she had made to go over the seats were also in the wash, and it was very uncomfortable sitting on those. All the tiny horses' hair would prick the back of your legs and thighs; it was all right for the boys they had thick trousers on.

Later on mum had a gas copper it would have a piece of copper pipe running along the side of the gas cooker. On the end was a small tap that enabled you to fit the gas copper pipe into it, that made the washing day a little bit easier it even had a small rubber wringer fitted to the top, at one time I also remember she had a gas iron that fitted into the same connection, but it was rather heavy and she preferred her electric iron. The only trouble with that was there weren't any power points. All the electrical connections were made from a three-way switch, from the one centre light in the ceiling. As well as the light bulb, you would also have the radio plugged into it. The lead would trail across the ceiling, and into the corner of the room where the radio was placed. As she plugged in the iron and started ironing the radio would then start to crackle, and the lampshade with its fringe would start to sway back and forth as though it was one of those Hawaiian dancers with their grass skirts on.

Some of the washing would have course been starched, such as tablecloths, sheets, pillowcases as well as dads collars. Men's shirts in those days came with detachable collars and dad would always have two fresh collars on every day, plus two fresh handkerchiefs which were also lightly starched, one for his pocket and the other one folded into fancy points to go into the top pocket of his jacket. He always liked to look quite smart, his clothes would be brushed down before he went out of the door, shoes brightly polished, and his watch and chain stretching across his waistcoat pockets. When he put his topcoats on someone would always have to help him by holding the collar and making sure all his clothes were smooth underneath. Most men in those days would also place their trousers underneath the mattress overnight making sure they were nicely pressed by the morning.

Once a week a friend of mums would come for coffee, we would have to go to the corner shop to buy a small tin of 'café- au- lait'. It cost sixpence a tin, and it just made two or three cups of coffee. She also baked a cake, which we dare not touch until the visitor had gone. Apparently, it was bad manners to serve a cake to visitors that had been cut. The little table would be laid in the front room with her best tea service, it was the one that she had been given as a gift for her silver wedding and it was always kept for best. As was the front room, it was only used on high days and holidays. At one time I remember she had saved enough green shield stamps to get a pretty pink glass tea service which we were able to use that everyday.

The front room was quite nicely furnished really for those times, we had a brown 'Rexin' three piece suite, with brown velvet cushions, either the piano or the organ, a 'what-not' stood in the corner with little ornaments on it. On the mantle piece was a large wooden clock, a couple of photos and on the wall above the clock was a large print of Jesus sitting looking down on Jerusalem. I can always remember that picture, as the artist had given him such beautiful hands. There were two more large religious prints in large black ebony frames, plus mums Aspidistra on a stand in the window. Every week she would polish its leaves, and make sure it was alright, and depending on the weather, it would spend a little time in the garden catching the sun or soft rain, as you went past the front room window it would look as though some Red Indian was hiding behind the net curtains. *(Because by the time I grew up and inherited it, it only had one leaf!)*

We also had a mirror in the back living room over the mantle piece. As we got older we would stand in front of it to do our hair, and put on our makeup, but you had to be careful of not standing to close to the fire. If you did some times the draught coming through the door would cause the bottom of your dress to be pulled up the chimney. You had to be pretty smart to quickly step back.

Summer time also meant Carnival time. It's my belief

that all the monies collected at the carnival went to help support the new General Hospital which had only been opened a couple of years. Elsie was one of the guides in the Guard of Honour when one of the Royal Duchess's came to open it, the hospital would place a couple of floats in the procession, manned by the doctors and nurse's who worked there they would hold out bed sheets, bedpans, white enamel buckets and anything that held money. The crowds of people watching would be very generous and throw money into the receptacle and if it missed it didn't matter. All the people walking along beside the floats had tins with *'Support your local hospital'*, written all around it. They then picked the money up and placed it into their tins which they also rattled away encouraging the crowds for their money.

There was no National Health Service back then. A visit to the doctors would cost a couple of shillings plus the medicine that he would make up in his own dispensary. Hence, the yearly appeals for support. Some people would pay a penny a week to belong to the hospital scheme whereby if they were sick and had to be hospitalised their penny would help towards the cost of the care. *(Many years later in 1972 my own daughter Maureen, who was a student nurse at Southend Hospital, would be on the floats and she carried the bedpan to collect money).*

The procession would stretch for a couple of miles and be really spectacular, with lots of bands playing all sorts of music from brass to jazz. Sometimes we would even have the 'Dagenham Girl Pipers', they were very popular with their Bagpipes and drums. This band was so well known that it would also travel abroad so we were lucky to get them. There would also be loads of clowns some riding on 'penny farthing' bikes, some walking along on stilts. And some just walking along juggling balls in the air.

People dressed up in their uniforms such as The St Johns Ambulance Brigade with their large white belts around their waists and across their chests. The Girl guides and Brownies, Cubs, and Boy Scouts, would all marching along waving their flags and banners. The representatives' from all of the trades people in the town such as the Coal Merchant, Diary producers, and Uncle Tom Cobbly and all; The Carnival Queen with her crown, and all her ladies in waiting, Plus the carnival Queens and their ladies in waiting from the surrounding Towns and Villages. They had all been selected from the Local beautiful girls of their respected town or Village, everybody would all get together to support our local Hospital.

The whole town would have something going on every day of the week. On the last Saturday night of the carnival, all the hotels and the Kursaal would hold a Carnival Ball, where all the 'toffs' of the town would gather; The Ladies in their Evening gowns and the men in their Black suits, starched shirt fronts and bow ties.

But the best part for us children was the carnival fair. I'm sure, if we had found enough empty bottles we would have been up there every day. However, mum and dad would take us on the Saturday night. It was magic. The lights, the lovely carousel's riding on these beautiful wooden animals with the jolly music playing. The coconut shy, hoping you would win a prize, if only a gold fish, and all the time the clowns would be there encouraging you to go and see the side shows; The *'Bearded Lady,' 'The Fattest Man in the world', 'The Tallest Man in the world',* and so it went on. One year, our uncle Jack was down on a visit, and mum was thrilled to bits when he won some thing for her at the fair, it was the china cottage biscuit barrel she used to treasure. However that was a wonderful time. The town seemed pretty bleak after all that, but at least they would have raised a lot of money for the local hospital.

As the summer ended, so mum had to have the chimney swept, to get ready for the winter fires. That in itself was quite a performance. Before the chimney sweep arrived, every thing that could be moved out of the room was moved. Mirrors', all the pictures on the wall, plus the curtains and chair covers. Down the road would come the chimney sweep, riding his bicycle, with this one wheeled flat -bottom contraption fixed somehow to the bicycle on which he had placed his brushes, empty sacks, and all that he would need for sweeping the chimney. He was a tiny little man, his clothes I'm sure stood up on their own, which were so thick with soot. *"Come on in Mr Martin" Mum would say, 'straight through here',* I'm sure Mum only said all that hoping he wouldn't brush against the wall. Once he was safely inside the room with all of his equipment the door would be shut. She would tell us to go down to the bottom of the garden and shout when the brush comes out of the chimney,*" I want to make sure it's been swept properly"*. When the brush finally appeared, a great big shout went up, *"it's out Mum, its out!"* Then, with Elsie helping, and anyone else she could lay her hands on, she would start to wash and clean everything in the room. Even so, in doing all that, the smell of the soot would last the rest of the day.

The next big thing then was getting ready to go back to school. Leonard by this time would have left school and was working and fitted himself out. Elsie, Jack and me would all have to go up and see Miss Brown. She ran her little club business from her home, which was situated in Park Street. In, we would all go into her front room and out would come her tape measure. Elsie would be first to be measured up for a new gymslip, winter coat (provided of course that she had outgrown her old one), and shoes. Then Jacks turn, two pairs of short trousers, shoes and a jacket. Then my turn the same as Elsie, although if her old coat wasn't to badly worn I would have that. I was also able to have her old gymslips; everything had to be passed down. With the exception of shoes, mum didn't like us to wear each other's shoes. My brothers never wore boots in their lives, which, was the norm in those days, only shoes. Mum, would also, un-pick mens' trousers. Using these as a pattern, would make new trousers for Jack to knock about in.

Elsie and I would also have navy blue, fleece lined knickers, with a little pocket in the leg, supposedly for your hankie. Navy blue stockings, done up with a suspender hanging from your liberty bodice. Navy blue jumpers that mum had knitted, always with a yellow, red or green stripe around the neck and cuffs, and grey pullovers for Jack, and then we would be ready to start school.

Miss Brown's name suited her very well, she was just like a little brown bird, a very small rounded little lady. Once a week, you would see her riding a very large upright bicycle. Down the road she would come with her coat tails flying, and, a large money satchel placed across her shoulders. *'Its Miss Brown!'* we would shout to Mum, and into the house she would go and mum would make her a cup of tea and then pay her. I think it was about two and six a week for our clothes.

When I was little, I used to have a hot water bottle shaped like a rabbit, it was grey with long ears which you held it by. Mum would say to me, *'don't let Margaret see that rabbit';* if she saw it she would scream blue murder, she wasn't going to bed with that rabbit. So when Margaret stayed, the rabbit was put away. Instead we would have a big stone one with a cloth wrapped around it that was ok until you knocked your toe on it.

When we went to bed at night, we would have a candle, and in the shadow caused by the flickering candle. With our fingers we would make silhouettes on the bedroom wall, dogs wiggling their ears, a rabbit sitting upright, a horse and whatever else Elsie and Jack could think of. Then, as usual we would have a sing song and fall sleep. Elsie mentioned the other day, that a couple of the neighbours asked mum if her boys were in bed yet? To which mum replied, *"yes and all tucked up"*. *"I thought so we could hear them singing', "When you're riding the range in the sky" or "Waggon Wheels"*. The boys loved to sing cowboy songs and sea shanties. Later on in the war when he was away at sea, Len would sing his own version of, *"I Wanna be back home in Dixie",* which would be;

"I wanna be, I wanna be I wanna be back home in Pitsea"

To which I replied, *"But you don't live in Pitsea". He would say, "But Pitsea is the nearest place to home while I'm at sea".* When Jack was home as well, they both used to sing it all round the house.

As the winter approached, the coal man would start to make his regular appearance. Of course, he would still be around occasionally during the summer months, but in the winter, it was weekly. Up the road, he would come, with his lovely 'shire' horse pulling this big coal cart. The horse, somehow knew which houses to stop at. As the coal man delivered his coal, any bits of coal that dropped off, we would quickly gather up to take home. Sometimes, he would shout at us to put the coal down but more often we would get away with it. The best bit of all, was when the horse started to move, we would all jump on, or cling to the back, to have a ride. Of course, we would go home filthy, but with a few lumps of coal stuck down our pockets.

We would also have the 'rag and bone' man come down the road, with his horse and cart, shouting out, *"rag-a-bone, rag-a-bone"*. He would have coloured balloons, swaying from his cart, and if you gave him some rags he would give you a balloon. We would rush home, and tell mum, that the 'rag and bone' man was up the road and he had balloons and did she have any rags, to which, her smart answer would be, *"No, only the ones on my back"*. After a bit of, *"Oh, please mum"*! We would get some. Then, off we would go, chasing after the rag man to get our balloons, sometimes you would give him jam jars for a balloon.

This was also the time, when mum started making her *'cough syrup'*. God knows, what, she put into it, but it tasted and smelt lovely. She would collect all the pop bottles she could lay her hands on, and sterilise them. Then all the ingredients which, she had bought from the chemists would go into a big saucepan and simmered till it was ready to place in the bottles. She would give several bottles to Agnes and Olive to help them through the winter, Ted, especially would like it, and take a small bottle to work every day. He said it helped to keep him warm, and was good for his chest. Also, at this time mum would start bottling; Picked Onions, Mustard Pickle and Red Cabbage. She would save all her 2lb jam jars for this purpose.

During the winter months, when we couldn't play outside, as often as we would have liked. We would get a bit bored. Mum would sit down with us at the table, and teach us how to play cards, 'Patience, Snap and Sevens'. Or we played 'Snakes and Ladders', and 'Ludo'. She would even get us to cut out strips of cloth, this cloth came from swatches of men's suiting, and with this she would make her rugs, that would keep us occupied for ages. Cutting out these lengths of cloth, which had to measure approximately, one inch by four? Then she would teach us how to push this piece of cloth through this large piece of sacking and start making the rugs.

Most houses, in those days didn't have carpets all over the floors, they had Linoleum (Lino), and these rag rugs or small carpets would then be placed in front of the fireplaces, and by the bedsides; plus, small ones in the hallways outside each door, to keep out the draughts. The only large piece of carpeting was the stair carpet. That would be laid down along the landing, down the stairs, and along the hallways. It was grey corded stuff with a red or yellow line running down either side.

This Lino would have to be washed and then polished every week. You would do all this, on your hands and knees. The rugs would be placed on the washing line and beaten with a carpet beater. This was made out of cane. If mum could get hold of Jack, this would be his job, helping him, get rid of some of his surplus energy.

When Jim, Olive's husband was working for the 'Fuller Brush Company', they sold mops and a liquid polish. You would place this polish on the mop and go all over the lino. It would polish the floor plus leave a sheen. It saved being on your hands and knees, but woe betide you if you polished under the rugs, you wouldn't end up on your hands and knees, you would end up the other side of the room on your bottom.

As the end of 1938 was approaching, so it was time to prepare for Christmas. Most families back then would belong to a loan club or a Christmas club. They would pay what they could afford into this club each week, and at the end of the year they would be able to draw it all out. A bit like the poor mans bank I suppose, however with this extra money they would be able to buy most of the things they needed to make a good Christmas. The workman didn't get paid any extra also they wouldn't be paid until lunchtime on Christmas Eve. There was always a big rush to get the shopping done. The shops did stay open till late though. That is when, they would get the bargains. The butchers would sell their meat and poultry off at half price as would the greengrocers their produce.

The later part of 1938 saw things happening in Germany, which for the rest of Europe didn't bode too well. So, our government decided that, in the event of any hostilities breaking out in this country a little preparation was in order. They decided to organise the setting up of a civil defence, and home guard etc. Dad joined the Civil Defence and became responsible for the distribution of the gas masks, which Elsie informed me they were issuing as early as 1938. Maybe the grownups knew what was going on in the world, but we children were quite unaware that this would be the last peaceful Christmas we would know for another six years. In the meantime, we were busy making paper chains. These were made with strips of coloured paper, approximately one and a half inches wide by about eight inches long. We would all sit around the table with a pot of glue and a small paintbrush and make paper chains. When we ran out of glue, mum would make us some more paste, with flour and water.

The paper chains would then be strung all across the ceilings, in the living room as well as the front room, and the hallway. We would also have two fires going, one in each of the living rooms. Whether we had a Christmas tree or not I don't recall, but we did see Father Christmas. He visited us one year. It was Christmas Eve and Elsie, Jack, Len and I had gone to bed, really too excited to sleep, even though we had sung a few carols. Jack and Len would be in their room, and Elsie and me in the little box room. Suddenly, mum popped her head around the door, and said, *"There's someone to see you, but be quiet"*. When we got down the stairs, standing at the front door was Father Christmas. Just as children imagined him to be, he was dressed all in red, with a long white beard, and a large sack. He was the son of the minister of the Chapel we used to go to. He spoke to us nice and softly, and asked if we had been good children. Of course we said yes, even Jack! He then put his hand down into his sack, and brought out some presents. We all had little oval tins of 'Bluebird Toffees', and a long tin with a picture on it, that was full of chocolate. You could use the tin after, for a pencil box; plus, an apple, and an orange. We didn't have many oranges through the year, so to have one at Christmas was quite a treat. Although, in the front room, mum, would have bowls of fruit and nuts. I remember dad asking us to go down to the greengrocers, and ask him for a pound of mixed nuts, but not too many Coconuts!

The Chestnuts, would be placed on the coal shovel, and then pushed underneath the fire amongst the ashes. It was lovely sitting around the fire, peeling oranges, cracking nuts. Dad would pull out his little knife, which he kept in his waistcoat pocket on the end of his watch chain, and peel his apples. He would play the piano and he and mum would sing songs they had listened to when they used to go to the music halls. Of course, we would join in as well. We had heard them so many times, that we knew all the words. Some of the songs went back to the time when mum used to go to the music halls with her parents.

I don't think Agnes and Olive were there on Christmas Day, as there wasn't any transport running. Nobody worked on Christmas Day; they would be there for a while on Christmas Eve and again on Boxing Day.

On the sideboard, in the front room, as well as the fruit and nuts, would be mums homemade Christmas cake. As well as a little blue candy dish with a few sweets in it. This candy dish was one of the first Christmas presents that mum had from her grandchildren, Agnes had taken them into 'Woolworths', and they wanted to buy their 'nan' something. So they had bought her this pretty little dish, she kept that, in pride of place on her sideboard. Many years later she gave it to her eldest granddaughter.

The workmen at that time would have Christmas Day and Boxing Day off, but not New Years day; therefore we didn't celebrate it too much. The exception was in Scotland, they would just have Christmas Day off, and back to work on Boxing Day, but they would have New Years day off instead.

After the Christmas festivities were all over, everyone would settle down to the real world, of cleaning, washing and trying to keep dry and warm, especially getting out of a warm bed in the mornings. As soon as your feet touched the floor, you would start hopping around, hurrying up, to get something on your feet before they froze. Going over to the bedroom window, you would have to scrape the ice, from the inside of the window, before you could look out, to see what the weather was like outside. Sometimes, we wished that we could be sick, or something, then we could have a fire in the bedroom. How we longed for spring, so that we could play once more in the streets, and spend our days on the beach once again. By the time midsummer had arrived, so our lives would change, It would be six long years before we would be able to go onto the beach once again, and hopefully things would be back to a bit of normality.

Chapter Four

The start of World War II

During the spring and summer months of 1939, the countries of Europe were starting to get prepared in the event of war. Troops were being mobilised and several countries ordered their fleets back to homeports.

Our government had already set into motion organising of the civil defence, and home guard etc. As well as, making arrangements for the evacuation of the school children from out of the cities and large towns, to places of safety, they also started distributing loads of leaflets, with advice as to what to do, and where to go, in case of an air raid; *'How to make a gas proof shelter in your own home'*, and to start stocking up, an emergency supply of food and candles, and numerous other things. In London they were digging deep trenches and placing sheets of corrugated iron on the top People would then be able to use these trenches in the event, of an air raid.

All households and buildings were ordered to place wide sticky brown tape across their windows and the glass in the doors, in case of bomb blast. Every window and door had to have blackout curtains placed at their windows and doors. Not a gleam of light was allowed to be seen. Bicycle lamps and car headlights, and all public vehicles' had to have black painted shades placed on the top of their headlamps. If you light a cigarette, some would shout out, *"Put That B----y Light Out"!* It was a complete blackout. The 'Anderson' air raid shelters placed in the gardens would have an old blanket placed over the entrance, and around the shelter doorway were sandbags.

This total blackout was a nightmare, especially in the winter on a foggy night. If mum wanted anything at the shops, two of us would have to go. Mind, you could always find your way to the 'fish and chip shop', the wonderful smell would guide you there, the only thing was, once there, you had to feel around to find the door! *(Due to the thickness of the fog!)*

August of 1939, the Royal Navy took over the pier at Southend. Some of the naval staff was, already set up in the Palace Hotel, and along the Royal Terrace. So, for the duration of the war, the pier was out of bounds. By the time that war, was declared, the navy had increased their personnel. They included many Wrens, most of whom, worked on communications. All these smart young Wrens strolling around the town in their uniforms, it must have made the young men of the town sit up. They themselves were probably all below the age of seventeen, most of the over eighteen's had already joined up. Do you remember that song? *"They're Either Too Young or Too Old, They're Either Too Fast or Too Fast Asleep",* well that applied to our town at that time.

On the second of September 1939, the government had passed a bill for the compulsory call up of all men between the ages of 18 and 41. Agnes' sister-in-law Lil's husband Harold, had already gone. He belonged to the Territorial Army, and they had been called up a while before. Agnes' husband Ted, was called up, and he joined the Army, apparently during the first world war, he'd ran away from home and joined the army, he was only fourteen years of age. When his parents found out where he was, they had to buy him out, so he wasn't going to miss out this time.

Although dad was already in the civil defence, no way was he going to be left out. So, at the age of fifty-one, he went back into the Merchant Navy. Elsie was telling me about his first trip after the war had started. It was on a tanker and on their way home; the ship was badly shelled and became full of holes. To enable them to keep afloat and to make it back home, they plugged the holes up with cork and rope. And they made it safely back to port. She remembers it very well, because until recently she still had the birthday card for the 5th September, (her birthday) that he'd sent her, with the message, *" Happy birthday, money following, Love Dad"*. Although after nearly sixty four years she is still waiting for the money. *(The post must have been bad).* With his ship so badly damaged, dad had to wait for another ship, and so he went back to the civil defence and worked in a London hospital, in the mortuary.

On the 29th September 1939, every head of the household had to fill in a form with all the particulars of everyone living within that household. Next day they had to return the forms, and were then issued with Identity cards for every person living in the house. The food office collected up all this information and then sent you out your ration book. *(Food wouldn't be rationed, until the January 1940).*

Mum was a bit worried about the place where we were living. It was so close to the hospital, and also close by, was the boy's high school, with very large playing fields. From the air, it could easily have been mistaken for an army barracks, plus we weren't too far from the airport. In November the Germans flew over the town and were dropping mines along the river, of course the air raid sirens went, and at that time many people didn't have shelters to go into, so we went into the cupboard under the stairs until the *'all clear'* sounded.

As most of the schools had closed, education was practically non existent. It was fun at first, going into different houses a couple of afternoons a week, but that soon became boring. Then suddenly, education stopped completely, there weren't enough children or teachers left in the town.

The next time the siren went, Olive, Jim, and their two babies were staying with us. He was called up for the forces, and had to register. Because his job was in agricultural work, for the time being, he was exempt. When the siren went again, the lady next door invited all of us to go into her house. Her son had made her a gas proof shelter in her front room. I can tell you, it must have been a bit fusty in there. So many people all squashed up together. That was when they bombed Southend Boys high School; the bomb shook the foundations of the houses including ours. That was when mum and dad decided to move to another part of the town, hoping it would be safer.

We all walked up to see the damage caused to the school with the bombing, it looked as though it had dropped right in the centre, as that part was missing. There was quite a bit of activity going on, with the Fire Brigade, Home Guard and the Wardens all trying to clear away the debris.

Agnes and her sister-in-law Lil were a little nervous now that they were on their own, although they were most probably safer in Hadleigh. They asked mum if they could all come to her. Lil's husband, Harold, was already in France as part of the expeditionary Force, they had been fighting since they landed in France on the 11th September. Olive and Jim had already gone back to the country, and for the time they were quite safe. Of course, mum couldn't accommodate seven more small children and two more adults, but she had to do something to stop them worrying. People were already moving out of the town anyway, so that left lots of empty properties. She couldn't find a larger house, but what she did find, were two house's next door to each other that enabled the three families to move closer together.

There was a school still open, where we moved to, and Jack and I were both able to go back to school, if only for a short while. We hadn't been there too long when they decided to evacuate the rest of the children. They were sending lots of children abroad for safety, to Canada, Australia, and New Zealand at the time. Mum and dad were debating whether to send Jack and myself, but sadly, whilst they were making up their minds, the Germans torpedoed a British ship with hundreds of evacuee children on board. As with most parents, that put an end for the moment to the sending of their children abroad.

The school that Jack and I went to decided to evacuate, and the school was closed. The whole school and all the children went to Derbyshire including Jack; to him life was just a big adventure, with the exception of me, and a few others. I wasn't going anywhere.

In the meantime Agnes, Lil, and their seven children had all settled in next door to us. Dad was still working In London as part of the civil defence, as were hundreds of other people living in the vicinity of London where the bombing had already started. It wasn't quite as bad as it would be, once the *'London blitz'* started a couple of months later. The civil defence's job, was to clear all the rubble and dig around in the bombed out buildings searching for the victims. It wasn't a pleasant job, but most of the men and women were in their forties and fifties, and many of them had been in the first, world war. It must have brought back some horrendous memories for them

Air raids were still going on. At night, when the siren sounded, you would have to jump out of bed pretty quickly, rush downstairs and hide under the table, or in the cupboard under the stairs. Above you could hear the planes throbbing overhead, and the loud noise of the Guns. If you were brave enough to peep out of the door, you would see the search lights, sweeping across the sky, picking up the shape of the big barrage balloons. They were like huge elephants, floating about the sky. With the flashing of the antiaircraft guns as they fired at the planes, it was an awesome sight. In the mornings we would go out into the back garden, and pick up pieces of shrapnel, some of it would still be warm.

As Christmas 1939 approached, things were getting pretty bad, and London was beginning to be hit regularly. Of course, every time they made their way up to London, the sirens would sound here in Southend as well. To the German pilots the River Thames was a good road to follow, to reach their destination, which of course was London. Agnes and Lil's children would have to be woken up and got out of bed and rushed downstairs, and as you can imagine there were a lot of grumpy children around next day.

People would pray for a cloudy night. That's when *'Jerry'* probably wouldn't be over and we could get a good night sleep. However, if the moon was shinning and the sky was clear, mum would say, *"you wait he'll be over tonight"*, so we will all sleep downstairs. *"(They called it the 'bombers moon').* When the sirens sounded, the first thing, mum, and most other women did would be to grab hold of a large handbag. In this bag, would be all their precious papers, such as all the family's birth certificates, marriage lines, photos, ration books and identity cards, and insurance policies. One wondered if they grabbed their bags or their babies first.

Dad was working pretty hard up in London, and when he could get home he would tell the grown ups some terrible stories of what was happening in London. Most of the evacuees came home for Christmas. Dad went up to Derbyshire, to fetch Jack back home. It was also decided, that Agnes should take her children to Cornwall where they would be safe. Many of the countries in Europe had already capitulated, and the government was already giving out instructions, about what to do in the event of an Invasion.

Winston Churchill spoke over the radio telling everybody to defend their homes with whatever means they had. Mum had a First World War Bayonet in the cupboard. On hearing the speech, Jack went up and down the hallway brandishing this bayonet, and telling us all, what he would do to the Germans, if they came to our front door, he must have thought he was just like *'Errol Flynn'* in the film, *"The Three Musketeers."* Mum told him to behave himself and put it away before he did somebody some damage!

In January 1940 rationing began. The weekly allowance for each adult was; 2 oz, of Butter, Tea, and Cheese. Cheese would later vacillate, from 1oz to 4oz's. Margarine, cooking fat, bacon or ham, was 4ozs; Meat to the value of 1s 2p or by today's price 6p. Sugar was 8ozs, per week with a jar of preserves once a month. Our milk allowance was 3pts of milk per week, later on dried milk became available 1 can per month. We had I egg per week many people kept a couple of chickens in the back garden, as we did. We used to save all the potato peelings and cook it all up with some chicken food to make a hot mash for their breakfast.

We also had a point system whereby, once a month you were able to buy a tin of meat or fish. Those weren't the only things to be rationed. Coal, fuel, and water were also rationed. It was suggested for example, that upon taking a bath once a week, you only use five inches of water. Well you can imagine the laugh that caused, everyone trying to imagine Winston Churchill in five inches of water!

Sweets weren't rationed until July 1942. We were then allowed; 12ozs per month. Before they were rationed, they were very hard to find. If you saw a child eating sweets, you immediately rushed up to them to ask where they had got them, or if you saw a queue, lined up outside a shop you would join it. It didn't really matter, what they were selling, you wanted some, although if there was any sugar going spare Elsie would make us some toffee. If there were any apples around, she dipped them into the toffee, and made toffee apples.

Bread wasn't rationed until 1946, but it was in short supply and you had to get to the shops pretty early to get in the queue. If they had sold out, by the time you got to the counter, you'd have to find another queue to join pretty quick. They also allowed you four cakes.

Coal, being rationed was in short supply, but sometimes you would hear that the Gas works had some Coke, so two of us were delegated to walk to the Gas works along the seafront, to see if they had any left. We would borrow someone's pram or barrow, and off we would go. It was quite a distance from where we lived in Westcliff, to Thorpe Bay. With a bit of luck you would arrive home with a big bag of coke. It was the custom in those days that when the housewives cleaned their fireplaces out in the mornings, they would empty the ashes outside their back gates into the alleyways. All these ashes and cinders formed a good foundation to walk on, instead of the mud. I can well remember mum sending me out with a bucket, to look for cinders up the alleyways. I was always lucky enough to find enough large cinders for mum to bank the fire up. Woe, betide you if you came in, and picked up the poker. *"Don't poke the fire"*, she would shout, *"that's got to last us all day"!* She would save any small boxes that the sugar or soap powder came in, and fill them up with coal dust to put on the fire, but as I have mentioned before, you daren't poke the fire. All of this rationing would continue long after the war was over; sometimes it would appear that we were worse off.

Dad had come home from London with railway tickets and travel warrants, for Agnes and her children to get down to Cornwall. Elsie went with her to help with the children. In those days what with the bombing, and the troops taking priority on the trains, it was an awful long journey. On arriving in Penzance they were met by our cousin Muriel, Agnes and her children went to stay at her house on the Trenere Estate. Muriel herself had two children, Joyce the baby, and David who was the same age as Irene, just turned two years of age. Elsie went to stay at our aunt Jane (dad's sister) at her house in Hayle. Muriel's husband like Agnes' husband was also in the army.

With Agnes, her family and Elsie all safe in Cornwall, that left just five of us at home, plus Lil and her three children still living next door. By this time, the local council had delivered us an air raid shelter, and it had been dug into our garden. It only held four people, so you can imagine how cramped it was in there, with us and Lil and her three children. Mum and Lil had difficulty climbing down into it, so ever resourceful; Jack decided he would make a ladder so it would be easier for them to climb down into the shelter. Before doing that however, he got one of baby Alan's (Lil's son) *'Ostermilk'* tins. Made a few holes all around it, and hung it up in the centre of the shelter with a candle inside. You were not allowed to have any lights in the shelter other than a torch. The only lighting you had was those provided by the searchlights and the flashes of the gunfire in the sky.

With me acting as his *'go-for girl'*, he managed to get hold of a large box and proceeded to make these steps. All went well, and he had everything in place, did a test on them, then called mum and Lil to try out his steps. Down the garden came mum and Lil, smiling happily, that they wouldn't have to struggle climbing in and out of the shelter any more. Once they were down on the bare earth, they praised him and said what a good boy he was. Poor Jack, as they attempted to get out, the steps collapsed, and mum pulled all the sandbags down on to herself and into the shelter. Fortunately no one was hurt, and mum said it wasn't his fault he had only tried to be helpful. She also told him to leave the light with the candle inside, as that would come in useful when we went down the shelter that night. As he lit the candle and we started to settle down, it was lovely to be able to see each other. All went well for a while, when suddenly our eyes started to sting, and we were all coughing and spluttering. We thought the Germans had dropped gas bombs; instead it was poor Jacks home made candlelight. With no air coming into the shelter, the smoke and fumes couldn't get out either. After that it was better to leave things as they were. One dinnertime when the siren sounded, the planes were flying overhead, the guns were banging away, mum shouted; *"Quick get down into the shelter"!* We all ran down into the shelter, as was the norm, the dog jumped in first, followed by the rest of us. When the *'allclear'* had sounded, we all trooped back into the house. Mum in her hurry had forgotten to turn all the gases off while the dinner had been cooking; she was met with a wonderful sight. The cabbage water had boiled over into the frying pan where all the sausages were floating on the top!

About six to eight weeks after Elsie went to Cornwall with Agnes, she came home. Mum wanted her home with us; she liked all her chicks in one place. Elsie was only fifteen, and the journey back through London was very dangerous. The bombing was getting worse every day. Auntie Jane had put her on the train with her sandwiches and sat her in a corner seat and told her not to move until she arrived in London. Poor Elsie, she was so timid, and not very worldly wise *(as most young girls were in those days)*, that she sat in that corner seat for approximately 12 to 14 hours, too frightened and shy to eat her sandwiches or go to the toilet. Good job like the Queen, she could hold her water.

Dad took us all up to London to meet her, except Len he was busy at work. Before we got into London you could see the devastation the bombing had caused. There was also a terrible smell of gas, dust and other things you couldn't define. We had to go on a bus across the city to reach Paddington Station, which had been badly hit, I don't remember if any air raids happened while we were in the city, but eventually mum, dad, Jack and I reached Paddington Station and met Elsie off the train. I bet she was as glad to see us, as we were to see her, and mum and dad had one of their 'chicks' back home.

All went well as we started our journey back home until we were standing at the bus stop. Mum said to Jack and myself; *"I don't want any playing about with you two, when the bus comes along, I want you to get on very quickly, and no arguing"*. Well the bus came along and doing what I was told, I jumped on the bus. So the bus went off with me on the platform, leaving all the others with their mouths wide open watching me disappear. I still stood on the platform thinking I'd get off at the next stop. Suddenly, there was a taxi racing along behind, with dad hanging out of the window shouting, *"stop that bus stop that bus! Stop that bus!*

My little girl's on that!" When the bus eventually stopped, dad grabbed hold of me, and bundled me into the taxi, and off we went back to the original bus stop. Of course Jack thought it very funny. You should have seen dad he said, hanging out of that taxi window shouting; stop that bus! Stop that bus! Just like one of the gangster's at the pictures, except he wasn't waving a gun. Trust Jack to think of something like that.

It was around this time that a bomb dropped in Liftstans Way, one of the German planes had been shot down. Mum and Lil decided to go for a walk to see the damage. Lil had her three children, in their pram, and with me in tow, off we went. It wasn't very nice really; there were the remains of the pilot's parachute hanging from a tree plus one of his boots. It wasn't a pretty sight, we didn't stay too long, it didn't seem right somehow, although we were at war, he was still someones son. We continued on to walk all along the seafront. There was barbed wire placed all along the promenade, so you were unable to get down to the beach. Maybe it was there to keep us in as well as keep the Germans out. As we continued our stroll along the sea front, we suddenly noticed a young man well ahead of us. He was sitting with his arms folded across his chest. His right foot resting nonchalantly on his left thigh and he was smoking a pipe. Immediately, Lil remarked to mum, *"Nan does that young man in front, put you in mind of anyone?"* When Mum looked up, she was off again, like one of Nelsons battleships', with her coat tails flying. Seized the pipe out of his mouth, and boxed his ears. As he stood up rubbing the side of his face, Lil said *"oh my gawd, it's Jack"!* By the time we reached them, Jack was walking away, with Mum telling him to go straight home and wait for his father. She said to Lil, *"he's taken the 'Ole Man's' pipe and stuffed it with tobacco, I'm going to have to watch that boy";* but she was grinning as she said it. He had just turned fourteen at the time. Poor Jack. Of course he got away with it, all dad said was, *"well he's just that age, to try things out".* But I seem to remember that later, dad filled a pipe for him and Jack, and they both sat down together. Dad made him smoke it, until he rushed outside, and was violently sick.

By this time, the situation in Europe was getting worse. Already Belgium had been overrun by the Germans. We had a few of the Belgium refugees in the town. Jack made friends with a couple of them, as boys do; they were the same age as him. I don't think any of them knew what each other were saying, but they mixed quite happily together. When Jack went out with them, I didn't go. I thought they were quite mad and too excitable. One of them chased me up the alley, and I didn't like that.

School for us children was still a bit spasmodic, and Jack got himself a job, although he was still only fourteen. It was selling 'Curtis ice cream', *"stop me, and buy one".* Poor Jack he did try, he got on the bike with the refrigerated box in the front, and decided to go over to the airport to sell his ice cream. There were lots of soldiers and airmen over there; naturally he thought he would do a roaring trade. Well he did come back empty, but not as he would have wished. Unfortunately when he arrived at the airport, the siren sounded, like everyone else, he had to go into the air raid shelter. There were German fighter planes overhead and they were machine gunning the airport. When the *'all clear'* finally sounded, he went to retrieve his bike and found it was empty. The soldiers and airmen had stolen all his ice cream, and that was the end of that job. He did get another job in 'St Anne's' wood yard, but he only lasted a couple of days. He told me recently, it was because he wouldn't call the boss, sir. *" When you are*

Knighted, then I will call you sir ", he said. So that was Jack out on his ears again

It was the middle of May 1940, and the situation in Europe was getting worse. Lil naturally was getting worried about her husband Harold. He had been over there since 1939 when the war was declared. Now, it seemed that what remained of our Army, and the remnants of what remained of the other European countries armies, were all gathering on a beach in Dunkirk France, with the hope of being rescued. Everybody seemed to be glued to the radio, listening to the terrible news about the plight of our armies. They issued an order that the government needed to requisition all small Boats, Tugs, and any other Vessels that they could lay their hands on and be commandeered by the Navy. They were ordered to take their boats to certain location spots, along the coast, and to register them. Then hand them over to the Royal Navy.

Many of the owners of the small boats, they included the fishing and cockle boats from Southend and Leigh, plus volunteers, all went with the boats to give what help they could in rescuing our armies. By the 3rd of June, the evacuation of Dunkirk was completed. They were very brave men and boys, who went over with their boats into a war zone. But in the end they managed to save 335,000 British and French soldiers, Harold was one of them to be saved. By this time Lil had already left the house next door, to join her in-laws, who were living out in the country, near Chelmsford. Lil waited for the news about her husband along with his family... Quietly, the army had already made a lot of, mock up guns, to place all along the coast, making out that we had lots of weapons left. In fact, we didn't have any. They even brought the old fashioned cannons out of the museums, we had nothing left, and everything we had was all left in France. The soldiers were all given leave, and told to make themselves be seen, so the spies (and there were plenty around), would report back to Germany. Of course there were only a token few left back in the barracks, but anything to fool the enemy.

After Dunkirk, it seemed that we were next on Hitler's list to be overrun. Things were looking very bad. Dad came home from London where he was still dealing with the victims of the bombing, and told mum that the Germans had been dropping petrol bombs in London, and the terrible sight of those poor victims was awful, and he wasn't going to have his family killed like that. So he had contacted 'Granma' and told her that we were all going down to Cornwall. Mum then, had to make arrangements as to what to do about her home and everything else. Good job Elsie was home to help her. The lady next door said she would store all her furniture, and anything else we couldn't take with us. Mum used to send her money each month for the storage. Len wasn't coming with us, as he was working and would miss his friends, also he was just eighteen. Before another year was out, he too would be back at sea.

We must have got the milk train, as when we arrived at Southend station it was still very dark as obviously the 'blackout' was still on. Half way through the journey, the train was diverted into a siding. A bomb had dropped on the lines ahead, and we had to stay on the train until the line was repaired. It was still dark, but by this time we were nearly into London. It really wasn't a good place to be stuck on a train; the searchlights were still roaming the skies, and the guns going off. By this time mum and dad were getting a bit anxious; we still had to get across London to catch the 'Cornish Riviera' train to take us to Penzance. There was only one train, a day to Penzance, which left the station at nine-o-clock in the morning. We did finally catch the train. It was an awful long journey, and we were all thankful to finally arrive at our destination.

We stayed for a couple of nights, at a friend of Cousin Muriel's. Dad found us somewhere to live, and it was in the same street that he had been born, Camberwell Street. The whole street apparently had been due for demolition, but due to the war and all the evacuees coming into the town the council had to quickly make them habitable. The interior of the house was exactly as I have described it in a previous chapter, of the house where dad had been born, except, there was now a gas cooker and a sink in what was the washroom, so you could use it as a kitchen. The kitchen range remained in the back living room for heating.

The local council also supplied each household with wooden camp beds and army blankets. Dad was soon up the council offices, demanding proper beds and bedding, he soon had them. Most of the people working there were either related to him, or he went to school with them. I started back to school, and dad went to see an old school friend. Her name was Lily and she said that Elsie could go and work for her if she wanted to, in her fish and chip shop. So Elsie started work. Despite the fact she often she came home smelling of the fish and chips, it meant that we were able to get extra fish, if there was any to spare. She was sixteen and it was her first job. Dad did the same for Jack; he got a job in the Penzance and District Coop: he had just turned fourteen. We hadn't been there too long when Len came on a visit. Everyone was so pleased to see him. The tea table was laid with as many goodies as mum and dad could get hold of, with things as they were, we didn't know when we would all meet again, so it was nice to make his visit as happy as possible.

It wasn't long after Len went back, that we moved. Dad had managed to get a larger house, in Penwith Street. It was only at the top of the road, and was an old bakery. The house still had the large flat fronted shop window, also the large shelf where they used to display the cakes. As you went into the front door, on your right there were stable doors leading into a small room that was the original shop. To the side of the shop was another stable door, which led into a back living area, and to the left of the living room was a cupboard type door, that hid the stairway to the next floor. Also leading off the living room, was a fair sized kitchen, and leading off the back of that, was a huge room, which was the old bake house. Set into the back wall was a big chimneystack, and the original bread ovens. The bake house took over most of the back yard, so that left a very small area in which to play, but the yard still contained an outside toilet and coal shed, and we still had that wonderful bake house in which to play. Upstairs were three bedrooms, a bathroom and toilet, and another set of stairs leading up to a huge attic. Like the bake house, it was a wonderful play area for us children on a wet day.

Now that we had more room, Agnes came to live there as well. The children used to have wonderful times playing shops, and sitting on the shelf in the shop window and watching the world pass by. The attic window also had a window seat, one that you could curl up on. When the Germans were bombing Plymouth, you could see the reflection in the sky. It must have been horrendous, just slight sounds echoing across the water, and the flashing lights in the red sky. If you have ever been to an outdoor concert at night, and they play *'Beethoven's' 5th Symphony'*, usually they have a big firework display at the end, while the orchestra is reaching a crescendo. Well that's what the bombing of Plymouth looked like. This was for real; one can only imagine the suffering that was going on. In the daytime of course, we had a wonderful view of St Michael's Mount, and any boats that happened to be in the bay.

Many people had moved down to Penzance from London to get away from the terrible devastation that was going on. A few of them came to live in the houses opposite us in Penwith Street. Like us, they only arrived with the clothes they stood up in, plus a few suitcases with any treasures they could rescue. One of the boys who Jack made friends with, even joined the home guard, so that he would have something to change into when he came home from work. I think his name was Ernie or maybe Harry Hughes. I had made friends with their sister Lizzie. It was a scream, when he came home from work and changed into his uniform, he would lounge against the brick wall of his house, legs crossed, hands in his pockets, cigarette dangling from his mouth, and his battle dress open down the front . Well you can imagine how we kids would tease him, shouting out *"lookout the Germans are coming let's all get behind Harry or Eddie (whatever his name was) he'll save us"!*

An elderly lady happened to be sitting on a kitchen chair outside her front door one day. I had never seen anyone sit outside their front door before, and thought it rather strange, but apparently it was quite common in London and other large towns, when they didn't have a back garden to sit in. Soon after she had moved in, dad came and asked mum for some clean strips of white bandages, (we had to make our own out of old bits of sheeting, and bandages were unavailable). He also wanted some bread, boiling water and a bowl. Of course, she wanted to know what he wanted all that for. He told her, that the lady who was sitting outside her front door was in terrible pain, with a big 'carbuncle' on the back of her neck, and he was going to put a bread poultice on it for her. Nobody else would touch her as she was so dirty. He said that the house smelt, as did she, that nobody would go near her. Well, he went over to her twice a day, with his bowl, boiling water, bread, and bandages. Eventually he came home and said to mum, *"Its burst, you ought to come see it, its left a hole in her neck as big as my thumb"*. Of course, mum declined, and said *"no thank you very much; you just get on with it."*

Of course that wasn't the end of dad's good deeds. The next thing is, he came in and asked mum if she had any toothcombs, which of course she had. We used them to go through our heads when our hair was washed. Next thing is, in he comes with some children in tow, and tells mum he wanted her to get the fleas out of the children's heads, as they were lousy. Well you never saw mum move so quickly, she bundled all of Agnes' children, and myself into the back living room, and told us to stay away. Well we did stay out of the room, but they had forgotten about the stable door, so I opened the top half, and Margaret, Phyllis and I were able to see what was going on. There was Agnes, mum, and Elsie, each, with a toothcomb in their hand, combing these children's hair over spread out newspaper. Dad by this time of course, had disappeared. After a while, one of them said, *"I can't do this any more, its making me feel sick"*, to which mum replied, *"Well I expect these things are making these children feel sick as well."*

When one considers the trauma these children had to endure over the past months during the blitz in London, sleeping on the platforms in underground stations, Anderson shelters, or any other shelters that may have been available, night after night and sometimes during the day. Never knowing what awaited them, as the *'all clear'* sounded, whether they would have any homes to go back to. Many times there wasn't, and sadly their homes weren't the only things they had lost. But now for a time they were safe in Penzance, and they were alive and well, so what did a few fleas matter.

Agnes' children went to their grandfather's old school St Johns, and like his grandfather, forty-five years previously, his eldest grandson David would also begin his education at St Johns. The school was quite near. From outside our front door you could hear the children playing in the schoolyard. At the bottom of our road tucked away in the corner, was an old fashioned shop, and on their way to school the children would go in there hopefully to buy some sweets, but many times they were in short supply. Sweets as I have mentioned before, were finally rationed in July 1942, when we were allowed 12 ozs. Per month; so of course, until that time, we always had our ears and eyes open when we saw a load of kids running. So with a few pennies clutched in our hands, off we would go to join any queue that we could see, in the hope that at the end of it there maybe a few sweets

Little Rene, who wasn't quite three at the time, would love to sit on the top step outside the house watching the rest of the children playing. One day, she must have followed them up the road and decided to do what they were doing, which was climbing the railings and swinging their legs through the bars. Of course, she was so small; she became caught on the railings and couldn't lift her chin off the spike. You can imagine the screams. My friend Lizzie and I were also playing near them. We rushed over, and being that much taller than the others, managed to lift her off. She had cut herself and there was blood, so when I carried her indoors there was a right panic. After it was cleaned up, it wasn't as bad as it first appeared. So if you have a little scar just under your chin against your jawbone Rene, you can just say that it is your 'war wound'.

Agnes hadn't seen her husband Ted since he had his last leave. He went to visit her and the children in Penzance, and that was when she had a family photo taken in a studio, of Ted and her, and the four children. I believe he was stationed in north Wales somewhere and managed to see his parents frequently. So off she went leaving the four children with mum and dad. I think it must have been one of the first opportunities she'd had to go away on her own.

It was after the episode with the evacuees, dad decided, that something needed to be done to make them more welcome in the town. So to quote an article in the local paper of that time is as follows:

Quote
"Civic support is being given to an effort in Penzance to provide 700 evacuee children in one of the parishes in the borough with a Christmas party.

The idea was conceived by Mr W, J, Nicholls, who, returning to his native town after 25 years absence as a Chief Steward in the mercantile marine, felt that hard words had been said about the town in the matter of the evacuees, and that an opportunity should be given to Penzance to show its true hospitality.

The idea immediately found favour, and a committee has been formed among the patrons of the Cornish Arms Inn to give a party to the 700 hundred evacuee children in St John's parish.

Mr Nicholls is Hon, Secretary of the Committee, the licensee, Mr Uren, is Hon: Treasurer and Mr J Tonkin is Chairman. Among the most zealous workers on the committee are two Londoners. Messrs' Laban and

Mizon.

The vicar of St Johns, Rev, A, G, Coombs is giving the effort his full support, and has promised to place the large parish hall at the disposal of the committee free of charge.

Entertainment has been arranged, and a local dance band has offered its services free. The proposal is to have a Christmas tree on which there will be a gift for every child present.

The Mayor and Town Clerk of Penzance, Ald, J, Birch, and Mr R,C,E, Austin, have written expressing their pleasure that the scheme has been launched , and wishing the committee the best of luck in their efforts.

Voluntary subscriptions to the fund so far amount to £7 pounds. One of the gifts is a Kruger sovereign which will be auctioned for the fun
<u>Unquote</u>

Dad and the rest of the committee worked very hard to raise money for the event. Writing to the mayors of each borough from which the evacuees had come. One sent his appreciation for all that was being done, and promised to start a fund to raise a little bit of money. Another also sent his appreciation and a donation of £2... Letters requesting that messages of good wishes be sent to the Children were declined, although the letters were acknowledged, both by the King and Queen, and number 10 Downing Street.

Penzance did them proud, it was a lovely party. As you can imagine with 700 children, plus all the adults who were helping, the hall was pretty full. The tables all had white cloths, and white china. Plenty of plates full of cakes and sandwiches were placed down the centre of the table. There were loads of adults around to make sure that everyone got their fair share, and that the bigger boys didn't grab too much. We all had paper hats, the hall was decorated with balloons and paper chains, there was a Christmas tree in the corner with boxes filled with presents all around it, and Father Christmas was there. Although you could see, that the bigger boys were a little bit scornful of that. After the cups of tea were poured out, we then started on the goodies placed in front of us. Someone had donated a load of jellies and Ice cream.

Can you imagine 700 children eating and talking all at the same time? If there had been any music playing, I'm sure nobody would have heard it. They took pictures for the local paper, but unfortunately a very large man stood in front of Agnes' children, and me. I stood up on a chair, and looked over his shoulder but Margaret, Phyllis and David were too small. Irene was sitting on her mother's lap, so unfortunately we can't see them.

As the party wore on, and all the food had disappeared, so the band started to play. We had a lovely sing song of all the popular songs of that time; *"Run Rabbit Run", "Underneath the Spreading Chestnut Tree", "We're Going to Hang out the Washing on the Seigfried Line", And "The Lambeth Walk".* As usual there was a parody sang of course to the *"Lambeth Walk"* and it went something like this;

*"Hitler's brown shirt looks so fine,
Hanging on the Seigfried Line:
Streicher is in Jail,
Doing the Lambeth Walk. Oii!"*

There were nine verses to that ditty so of course I can't repeat all of them.

After all the presents had been given out, by Father Christmas, the tables and chairs were stacked away and the dancing started. Dad had the first dance with mum, and then he twirled Agnes around the floor, then Elsie and me. But while we were dancing we were also getting instruction. *"Hold your head up, keep your back straight, and don't look down, at your feet"*. I soon joined the other children dancing and jigging around in another part of the hall.

It was a lovely party. Dad and the rest of the helper's had worked very hard to make it a success. The only problem was that afterwards anyone having a problem would always seek dad out to help them. Dad had several names, to mum, he was always Will, to us he was dad, to his grandchildren he was 'Pops', to his uncles and other relatives in the town he was 'Boy Willie'. But to people that needed help he was Bill. I'm sure that if they had held any local elections they would have voted him in as their Councillor.

The Christmas of 1940, was a little bit different from the previous one. For the first time, we didn't see Olive, Jim and their children. They were still living down in Essex. There weren't so many toys, fruit or sweets around. If you were lucky the greengrocer allowed one orange per child, if he hadn't already sold out by the time it was your turn in the queue. If he had, you would quickly have to find another one to join. Mum and Agnes were wise, and they went off in different directions to join all the queues, so we didn't do too badly. I can remember that year; we all had pretty handkerchief cases. They were pink and blue trimmed with a little lace. I don't think we had any handkerchiefs to put in them though. Still they helped to fill a stocking, which wasn't as full as in other years. We were lucky really, with all the connections that dad had in the town we fared reasonably well.

It was about in the springtime of that year that we were bombed. We children were playing in the street at the time although there were several adults around either walking up the road or chatting. Suddenly we heard these planes overhead. On looking up to the sky, we saw what appeared to be four parachutes leaving the plane. Our immediate thought was that we had been invaded. As they came closer, there was a big scuffle in the street as everybody disappeared. They were not soldiers at the end of the chutes, they were bombs. By that time, I was the only one left in the street. I can remember banging on somebody's door to let me in, and then mum came out of our front door and dragged me in. There was one big explosion, and loads of dust and debris flying around, and for a few minutes there was silence. Everyone was waiting for the other bombs to go off, then there was movement with loads of noise, sirens, ambulance's, fire engines and police cars all sounding their sirens. The air raid warden's blowing their whistle's, telling everyone they had to get out of their homes, and leave the area.

Dad came home and the neighbours kept asking him what they should do as they didn't have anywhere to go. His reply was, to tell them to collect a few things in a bag and to stay put, while he went off to see where we all should go. After a while, he came back to say that everyone who didn't have any where else to go, should go along to these big empty house's along the esplanade, where someone would meet them. He told Agnes to get some things together and to go to Cousin Muriel's, she would be safe there and he would let her know where the rest of us would be. Mum then said she wasn't going anywhere, as Jack had gone missing. Dad then told mum to get going with Elsie and me, and he would go looking for Jack.

Apparently they weren't bombs, but land mines and only one had gone off. There remained three unexploded ones and they were waiting for the bomb disposal squad to arrive, possibly from Plymouth so we didn't know how long we were going to be billeted in these temporary accommodations. So off we went, leaving dad to search for Jack. He first went to Alma Terrace, as that is where the mine dropped and exploded. It was also where Uncle William Henry lived. Uncle William Henry told dad that Jack had been there helping people, and also helping removing the debris, but after a while he had told him to go home as Jack was getting a bit upset. Dad eventually found him, and took him back to the billet where we were all staying.

Dad told mum not to moan at him, as he had been a good lad and he was a bit upset and very tired after what he had seen. He frightened the life out of her later, when he told her he had got very tired, and needed a rest, so he sat down on what he thought was a milk churn, instead of which, it was one of the unexploded mines. Of course being Jack, nobody believed him. It was just one of his tall stories, although it was true about him helping in Alma Terrace.

There wasn't any furniture in these rooms, where we were billeted. They must have thought we all were going to sit and sleep on the floor. Until dad went off to the Town Hall to complain, and demanded that they give everybody a *'palliasse'* and a blanket, everybody soon had one. The next complaint was in the Pavilion where we had to get all our food. Evacuees complained to dad about the price's they were being charged. I remember on one occasion we were sitting down having our tea, up came a couple of men with a piece of cake in the palm of their hand, and said to dad, *"hey! Bill what do you reckon to this piece of bl----dy cake then"*. They started moaning about the size and price of this fruit cake, calling them all the thieves going. Off went dad to see the manager, and had a word with him about it. He told dad that the charges had come from the town hall and had nothing to do with him, whereupon dad told him to wrap up the piece of cake, and off he went to the town hall with these other men following him. Before they got back to the pavilion the prices had changed and everything came down in price.

A couple of the men who went with dad told everybody, *"you ought to have seen Bill, he told them how much profit they were making out of the things they were buying and then selling to us"*. What those people didn't realise was, that it was dad's job to buy and sell and make a profit, especially with food, and he didn't have to use a calculator *(they weren't heard of then)*. He had a wonderful mathematical brain so of course was very clever with maths, he could tell you the costing and profits before you could practically finish the question.

Elsie also remembers going with Agnes, and creeping down the side streets hoping to get into our house for extra clothing and bits for the children. She said it was really eerie trying to dodge the soldiers and warden's, guarding the streets, but it didn't last too long. Once they had cleared the bombs we were allowed home.

Elsie said that we were bombed out twice. The only thing I clearly remember is coming out if school one afternoon, two fighter planes flying out to sea, turned around and machined gunned us children as we all rushed out of school. Teachers started blowing their whistle's to get us all back to safety. Whether anyone was injured I don't recall.

Possibly it was all the bombing and being machine gunned, plus poor little Phyllis developing Rheumatic Fever that the decision was made to come back home to Southend. Mum wrote to Len, and asked him to look for somewhere for us to live. In the meantime, poor Phyllis was lying in bed with her legs covered in a

'Kaolin poultice' and then bandaged. She was in so much pain, this poultice was heated up on the stove twice a day, and then applied very warm to her legs. Her legs were then bandaged from top to toe. The doctor had advised Agnes to take her back to her own county.

Shortly after this we left Cornwall. According to Elsie, dad had already signed up for another ship, and was back in the merchant navy. At fifty-three years of age, he didn't have to go either. He was either very brave or very stupid, or maybe a bit of both. We went to stay with Olive and Jim in a place called Margretting near Chelmsford. Agnes went off to the other side of Chelmsford in a little place called Great Waltham. She stayed with her sister-in -law Lil who recently had a new baby, Terence David.

While we were at Olives and Jim's, we got a taste of country living. Watching Jim driving the herd of cow's in to get ready for milking. Olive giving me a jug, to go down to the milking shed and ask Jim for some milk. Whilst walking with Pat in a pram, all through the country lanes with Olive, to meet Pam from school. Jack trying to teach me to ride Jim's big bike, and then dumping me in a bed of stinging nettles. Olive then telling him off for putting me on the big bike. Elsie said she remembers Olive taking her in to Chelmsford on her sixteenth birthday. Olive and Jim had paid for her to have her first 'permanent wave' for her birthday. I can remember going with the family into Chelmsford and dad all dressed up in his uniform, and all the service men saluting him.

In the meantime Len had found us a house and off we went to see Agnes and Lil out in Great Waltham and spend a couple of days with them before moving back to Southend. They were all living in a little cottage, two rooms up and two rooms down, no kitchen or bathroom. They had to pump their water up from a well, which was also shared with two other cottages hidden from view behind high bushes and trees. The toilet was also way down in the garden, a bucket toilet which they had to empty in a cesspool. Mum, Lil and Agnes would often reminisce about that place. The biggest laugh off all was the story of Lil sitting on the toilet. Suddenly, the door which, was only hanging on one hinge, blew down. At that moment, the postman was passing by, heard the noise and said *"good morning Lil, everything all right?"*, *"yes, thanks postman"*, she replied, *"Have you any mail for me today?"*, *"no not today"* he replied. I bet he had a good story to tell when he went back to the depot.

Mum got most of her furniture back that had been stored, she reckoned there were a few pieces missing but never the less she'd got most of it, and we moved into Wenham Drive. Jack got a job with the 'London Co-op', and Elsie being sixteen, had to register for work. She got a job in munitions, working the other side of town. Len was also back in the merchant navy, and I went back to school.

We all soon settled down to living back home, taking no notice of the sirens sounding, unless we could hear the planes overhead. If we did, we just went downstairs, and went into the cupboard under the staircase. It wasn't too long before Agnes and Lil decided to come back as well. They all lived together in an upstairs flat above a second-hand shop, which came in very handy if you were replacing any bits of furniture. If the sirens went, they were all invited to share the elderly shop owners' shelter. It was a *'Morrison'* shelter, built like a large steel table, with wire mesh all around it. All the eight children would go into that. Everything was ok, until young Mickey, Lil's eldest son, during one air raid helped himself to the couple's Sunday roast, which was all ready for their dinner. There were ten of them in that flat, with steep steps, going down into a bit of garden with hardly any room to hang washing out. Mum used to say to them, that while there were still a lot of houses remaining empty, they should take the opportunity, and find somewhere with a garden and space for the children. Well Lil did. She moved to a nice little downstairs flat in Fairfax Drive with a garden. Agnes went to an upstairs flat in Gainsborough Drive that had a nice big attic bedroom. They were both living within a few minutes of mum, and would meet at mum's most days.

Once a fortnight, mum would be waiting for me as I came out of school, and off we would go down Hamlet Court Road. She would go first into the post office and draw the allotment that dad had left her, and then we went shopping. The best shop for me was 'Woolworth's' sweet counter. They always seemed to have sweets. I thought I had died and gone to heaven when she told me I could choose what sweets I wanted. I always chose 'Banana Splits', maybe not tasting a Banana since the war started, but I still remembered the taste. But the oddest thing was she said they were all mine and I found that rather strange. I didn't have to share them with anyone. We had been brought up to share; maybe, we wouldn't be getting anymore half chewed sweets from each other's mouths. She hadn't forgotten Jack and Elsie. They had a bag each for when they came home from work. Sweets had been rationed in July 1942.

Years later, a friend of mine would relate how her mother during the war, would cook a load of parsnips. Then flavour them with banana flavouring, before pouring custard on top. Sounds revolting, but then you never did know what we were actually eating.

Elsie, after finishing a full day's work, would come

home, and then have to go back to the factory a couple of hours later to do fire watching. It was compulsory a couple of nights a week. She would come home in the morning, have a wash and something to eat, and go back and to do, a full days' work again. On the weekends and any free time, she had she would go out with her friends, either to the pictures or dancing. Something her elder sisters didn't do. Her makeup was still 'Ponds vanishing cream', face powder and lipstick, *(if there was any about)*.

Time went by in the usual way. Queuing for food and anything else that was in short supply. Un-picking old woolies, and skeining it around the backs of chairs before washing it, and then knitting it up again, into pixie hoods, scarf's, gloves, balaclava helmets, etc. for the children already for the winter. As though we needed to be reminded, the sirens still sounded when the planes flew overhead; maybe we were getting too complacent. We would ignore them many times, that is until the guns started to fire then we would go back under the stairs. We would also saved any little bits of soap, and place it in a jar with a little drop of water, that made lovely soft soap which we would use for washing our hair.

As another winter approached, mum started to think about Christmas. Hopefully Len would be home again, which would make things easier, but in the meantime preparations were to be made. With so many little girls around, Agnes' three, Olives two, And Lil's one, six in all, they all wanted a doll for Christmas, but there weren't any to be had in the shops, and so the back living room table became a hive of activity. With the muslin that she had saved from the meat that Len had brought home from sea, she cut out the bodies. They were then filled out with any pieces of clean rag, or bits of soft wool. They did sell dolls hard paper faces, which would then be sewn onto the front of the head. Then long strands of wool, would be placed on top of the head for the hair. I think that was also the year that they managed to find bus conductors set for David. He made his sisters, and anyone else who would oblige, sit on the stairs. He'd then walk up and down the staircase, shouting out, *"any more fares please"*. He would then give you a ticket, then ring the bell which was attached to the ticket machine, walk to the bottom of the stairs and ring for the pretend driver to start the bus, and then call out, *"anyone for the next stop!"*. That kept him amused for hours.

Clothes were hard to come by, it was the era *of 'make do and mend'*. Usually, it was who was up first, was best dressed. Shoes were very thinly soled and your feet would get very cold in the winter, especially waiting around for the buses that sometimes didn't arrive. We would put cardboard or newspapers in them to keep warm. Olive's husband Jim was very clever, he would cut out and sew dresses for both Olive and his daughter's, and they looked very nice.

As for stockings they were non-existent. Good job gravy browning was still available, they painted their legs with that, and then they would try and pencil in a straight line down the centre on the back of their legs for a seam, or get someone else to do it. You will have to use your own imagination to what they looked like when it rained. The girls who were in the forces and the land army, wore thick 'Lyle' ones, of course they didn't want to wear those when they went out to a dance or on a date, so out came the gravy bottle.

After the long dreary cold wet winter, it was wonderful to be able to look forward to the spring of 1943. Amidst all the debris of the bombs, to be able to see the trees in blossom, and the spring flowers peeping through, it was magic.

Dad was home, he had been sent on a cookery course in London. The purpose of which was, in the eventuality of the cook on board ship being killed that someone would be available to take over the feeding of the remainder of the crew. He used to bring home samples of things they had cooked that day, lovely fresh bread and dinner rolls, and soups, one of which was a celery soup, it was delicious. In future years he would make it every Christmas as our first course. His Granddaughter Maureen still makes it to this day.

As dad was home, everyone came around to see him, and we had a bit of a party. Olive's little girl Pat wanted to show her granddad how well she could dance. So dad sat down at the Piano, fingers tinkling along the keys, one foot on the pedal and the other one sticking out sideways. Pat was dancing around, a little bit of tap dancing, a little bit of ballet; I think it was a little bit of.

'Ginger Rogers,' and a little bit of *'Moira Shearer'*. Suddenly the keys came down with a slam, there was a big shout, and lots of *"OH OH my ********* foot."* Mum said *"don't upset the children. If you don't get that corn cut, I'll cut it for you."* After a while we all crept into the back living room, and there was dad with his trouser leg rolled up to his knees, his foot in a bowl of water, still moaning and groaning. We all looked down into the depths of the bowl, and there, nestling on the top of three of his toes was a big red pulsating corn. Of course everyone still looking down into the depths of the bowl were *'oohhing'* and *'aahhing'* But he did give Pat a big hug and told her he was sorry that he shouted, but that she was a lovely dancer.

During the war, there was Double British Summer Time that enabled the farmers to have more time getting in their crops. Agnes would sometimes take her children onto the farm to help pick the peas and potatoes. Olive out in the country with her children, would take her them gleanning. After the farmer had got all his harvest in, he would allow the local people in to glean his fields. That way she could gather up lots of corn to help feed her chickens. Most people kept a couple of chickens. Mum even had a couple; one of them was called *'Blackie'*. Every time she laid an egg she would come and peck at the living room window, until she had caught mums attention.

Elsie at this time was going out with a soldier, his name was Eric Holmes. He was billeted not far from where she worked. She hadn't been going out with him too long when he was sent out to the Middle East. She would regularly receive airmail letters from him, and one of brother Jacks favourite tricks was to open it wide and pin it up on the wall, *(he never read it, just the first line)*. Poor old Elsie would rush home at lunchtime shouting out; *"is there any mail Mum?"* as she came through the living room door, her eyes went straight to the mantle piece, where all the mail was kept. She would look so disappointed, until mum said, *"I thought something came for Elsie this morning, have either of you two seen it?"* Jack would then sweetly reply *"Oh, do you mean that one, that says, 'To my Only Dearest Darling You', I think the dog ate it"*. You could hear poor Elsie scream at the bottom of the road when she discovered it pinned up on the wall.

But that wasn't the worst of his mischief. Mum, Agnes and Lil had left the children with Jack and me whilst they went out shopping. That was ok, we all played happily together, until Jack heard them coming through the front door. He quickly picked little Allen up, (Lil's son), and hung him by his little trouser belt on the picture rail. He didn't cry at all just smiled. Of course it was Lil who first opened the living room door. You can imagine the screams when she saw her little boy hanging from a picture rail. He quickly dodged the clip she was going to give him. *"He liked it,* "he said, *"He could see everything from up there".*

We were very lucky really, having a brother who never came home from sea empty handed. Len always brought home plenty of food for mum. Whenever he was coming home, everybody waited at mums. He would roll up in a taxi with loads of boxes and canvas bags. One year he came home with a big stem of Banana's. All the little ones were there, including Lil's children, she was never left out in the sharing of the goodies. Len gave her little boy Mickey a Banana and he didn't know what to do with it, so Len gave each of the children a piece of the fruit and showed them all how to unzip a Banana. Their first taste was a joy to see. It really made you feel sorry for the little ones, for all those little pleasures they had missed.

Agnes son David would always be on hand to help his uncle Len in with his luggage. No one dare touch his suitcase, only David. Len would put that on the table and tell David to unpack it for him and any loose change he found was his. Well David was very careful taking everything out, but Len always made sure there was plenty of loose change in the bottom of the case. He went home with his pockets bulging with all the money he had found at the bottom of his uncles' case. Len would bring home things that we had forgotten about. Loads of lovely meat, the meat would be wrapped in butchers muslin that would came in very useful once it was washed. There would also be very large tins of fruit, and huge tins of butter, ham and bacon. The bacon was sealed inside tins, and layered in lard which mum would save and use for cooking. One time I can remember he even brought home a whole side of bacon. There would also be crates of eggs, and oranges and enough tins and packages to keep us going until his next trip home.

Agnes and Lil would both go home with their share of goodies, and mum would send someone over to Olive or go over herself, so she too had her share with the fruit and sweets for the children. Although she lived some distance away, she still had her share. Len would always bring back sweets for the children, such as big boxes of Hershey Chocolate bars from the States. Len being so generous made things a lot easier, helping to feed three families during those spartan times. He would also bring home parcels of clothing that his friends in America had given him to bring back for his sisters. In those days, America had a scheme called, *'Bundles for Britain'*. Well, we had our *"Bundle for Britain"* delivered personally. In the parcel would usually be some makeup, for Elsie and silk stockings, and later on, the first nylons. Before he went back to sea, Len would also leave money, he used to put it in a large vegetable dish that was kept on the top shelf of the dresser in the living room, and (Maureen has this now in her hallway with flowers in.) He told mum she was to use it if anyone in the family needed anything. That was her safety net. It came in very handy everytime poor Phyllis' illness flared up and Agnes had to have the doctor. At five shillings a visit, plus the medication, it was a bit hard on a soldiers' pay.

The summer evenings used to be lovely and long, not getting dark until 11 o-clock in the evening. One evening fast asleep in my bed, I was woken up by a lot of giggling and *'whoo'*, *'whoo'*. Opening my eyes, I saw my brother Jack and four of his friends leaning out of my bedroom window all 'cooing' and 'wooing'. Mum shouted up the stairs, to ask him what was going on. *"Nothing"*, he replied and off they went giggling like a load of little boys down the stairs. I decided to see what they were all looking at, and it was two young women in the downstairs flat opposite, they had the curtains wide open, and there they were prancing about in their *'cami-knickers'*. I then heard Jack say to mum, *"why can't I have the back room"?* I shouted down, *"no he can't, he only wants to ogle the girls at the back"!*

I think my brother Jacks' hormones must have been on the rise. It was just after that, that he got a job as a steward in the naval canteen, along the sea front. Mind you, he did look very smart. They had supplied him with a navy blue uniform with all the brass buttons on the jacket, plus a peaked cap with some sort of emblem on the front. If you didn't know any better, you would take him for a petty officer, and he was only sixteen. I'm sure he had plenty of fun down there with all the wrens.

As soon as Jack became seventeen, he kept on, that he wanted to go to sea. After talking it over with dad, and Len when they were home, and realising that the following year he would have to register for service anyway, mum relented, saying *"he may as well do what he wanted, rather than be forced into something he didn't like".*

Jack applied to go the training ship, 'The *Vindicatrix'* that was based in Gloucester. He was accepted, and down came, the money tureen from the top shelf. She sent off the fee, and gave him enough money to rig himself out with all the gear that he needed. He was the only one in the family that on his first trip to sea went fully geared up. On the of September 1943 brother Jack started out on one of the biggest adventure's of his young life, he was seventeen years and three months old.

Mum was getting a bit anxious, he'd only been gone

less than a week and she hadn't heard from him, but suddenly a letter arrived, and it went something like this.

"Dear Mum, Dad, and all,

Hope you are all well, I'm fine although hungry, I have made a few mates but we are all starving hungry, they get us up early in the mornings and we all go to breakfast, but the grub is horrible and not enough of it and we are all starving. We all go to bed hungry can you send us some grub?
Hope to hear from you soon, and don't forget the grub.

Love Jack

P.S. don't forget the grub hope to hear from you soon.

Not content with that, all around the edges of the envelope he'd written, *"Don't forget the grub, and don't forget the grub".*

Of course the letter was passed around the family, mum baked a cake, and made up a parcel with all the goodies that she could get hold of, plus his sister's gave what they had, and off this parcel went with images of their little brother Jack starving to death. After this, a parcel went off once a week, for the length off time he was on the training ship. Unlike girls, boys are just stomachs on legs.

He left the training ship in December 1943, and after two weeks leave, he was allocated a ship the *"Paparoa"*. She was brand new, and of course had to go out on sea trials before being taken over by the shipping company. As the ship sailed up the Clyde, he noticed that his big brother's ship was anchored out in the middle of the river. Len was on the *"Queen Mary"*. Len recollected later, that he noticed Jack's ship come in and lay anchor. As he was well in with intelligence, and the customs, they gave him a lift in their Launch and drew up alongside the *"Paparoa"*. I don't think anyone was more surprised than Jack to see his big brother climbing up the gang plank.

Mum was very worried like all mums of that time, with dad and both of her son's at sea. Everyday they would announce over the radio the number of ships we had lost and whether there had been any survivor's. So she was pleased when Len came home for a few days and was able to tell her that he had seen Jack and all was well.

Jim had just joined the Royal Air Force, so Olive and her two little girls were living just a few doors away. Everyone being on their own was expected to come for dinner and tea, Agnes and her children, Olive and her two, Lil and hers. At least we would all be together. We were still getting air raids and the sirens were still sounding night or day, but for now it was best to get on with the preparations for Christmas.

Olive decided that she was going to make the Christmas puddings and the cake. The table in our back room had a big white cloth placed on it, and Olive started to get all the bits and pieces together for the cake. We all had to help, washing the fruit, chopping up nuts. I found it a bit odd when she started to grate carrots, and horrified when she asked mum for some gravy browning. I went to mum and said, *"She's putting gravy in the cake"? "It's alright"*, she replied, *"She knows what she is doing"*. Olive used to have the *'Womens' Weekly'* magazine every week, and it always published recipe's, on how to make a cake, and Christmas puddings and other things in wartime.

It wasn't until much later, that I remembered that

mum used to have a large table spoon. It was burnt black. What she used to do was, when she made the gravy at dinnertime, she would put a heap of sugar on to it, and set fire to the sugar, until it had turned to a caramel. She would then stir that, into the gravy, to colour it. So Olive was right, she was just using bottled caramel to help darken the cake.

After the long dreary cold wet winter, it was wonderful to be able to look forward to the spring. Amidst all the debris of the bombs, to be able to see the trees in blossom, and the spring flowers peeping through, it was magic.

Although things may appear to have been dark and gloomy it wasn't. There was plenty of entertainment going on in the town. In Southend, and the surrounding area, there were approximately thirteen cinemas, which always had plenty of people queuing up waiting to get in. There were also, two theatres; the '*Palace theatre*', and 'the *Regal*' which was a bit *'risqué'*, especially if '*Phyllis Dixie*' was there. She used to do *strip -tease* with a couple of large Ostrich feathered fans, (not that we were ever allowed to go).

We also had plenty of lovely dance halls, and the pubs did a good business until the beer run out. They were like a social club. People would go there to meet their friends and neighbours, play a game of darts, and a have a good old moan off about which shops had things hidden under the counter, just to give out to their favourite customer's. When dad or Ted came home on leave they would always go and have a drink, mum Agnes and Lil would also go along, leaving me and Elsie if she happened to be home to look after all the children. One time when Ted came home, he would regale them all, with the story of, "*The Battle of Lampeter*", where he was based at that time. He said how glad he was to be home, and how every night a big battle would go on in the town, fighting from bridge to bridge, and really having to struggle, until some one said *" I didn't know the Germans had invaded this country?" "They haven't "*, he replied, *"the town is full of Yanks, and we have to do battle every night to see who will get to the pubs first before all the beer runs out,"*, that would cause great hoots of laughter in the Local.

The radio though was our main source of entertainment. We had loads of comedians, such as; *Rob Wilton, Aurther Askey, Richard Murdoch, Flanagan and Allan, Tommy Handley,* with, *"It's that man again show"*. He was supposed to be a posh bloke speaking on the telephone, when suddenly you would hear a door burst open, and his Mrs Mopp would shout out, *"can I do yer nowh sir!, can I do yer nowh!"* That saying became very popular, especially with the kids and young girls. If they saw a lorry load of soldiers they would shout out, *"can I do yer naah sir, can I do yer naah!", "any time darling, any time", was* the reply. Of course they made sure the soldiers were still on the move, but that caused lots of laughter in the streets. We also had a comedy pair, by the name of, *" Old mother Riley and her daughter Kitty"*, many of these comedians also made films, which people would queue up to see, they caused a real laugh.

We also had dance bands with *Victor Sylvester* and his *'Come Dancing'*, *Billy Cotton* at the 'Hammersmith Palais-de-dance'; Loads of crooners and singers, music halls, and Sunday night theatre. They would tell such wonderful creepy plays, so good, you would be too frightened to go up the dark stairs to bed. The best one of all was *'Valentine Dyall'* with his *'Man in Black'* series. So, as you can imagine, we had lots of things to keep us all going. They also had *'Forces Favourites'*, with, *Cliff Michelmore,* who was somewhere with the troops, and *Jean Metcalf*, who was based in London. This programme would be relayed on Sunday lunch times. They would send messages from the boys to their loved ones back at home, with a favourite song. Their families back in the U.K would do the same from London. After the war was over, both, Cliff and Jean met for the first time, and were soon married. A happy love story, that began on the radio. All during the week, we also had, at lunch times, *"Workers Playtime"*, which would be relayed throughout the land for the factory workers. So you can see that, the *B.B.C.* did their best to keep our morale up.

Agnes had got herself a little job a couple of days a week. It was the first job she'd had since being married. When necessary, she would bring the children for mum to look after. She didn't mind housework, but when her sister Olive decided that she would do the same, it was a different kettle of fish. She hadn't been out to work either since her marriage, and had never gone out to do housework. She too, like Agnes, would fly in, leaving her two daughters Pam and Pat with mum. It didn't last long. She came rushing in one day, and mum, all alarmed said to her, *"what's wrong"*, *"that's it"*, she said, *"I'm not going there any more, do you know what that woman did, she'd put a half-a-crown under the carpet so I've nailed it into the floor she can stick her job"*. She did try again though, but wasn't lucky there either. The next one, the woman had left the cats mess on the floor, so Olive covered it with a piece of paper and left the woman a note, which told her in know uncertain terms what she could do with her job. As you can guess we all roared with laughter.

It was the spring of 1944, the spring flowers were peeping through, the trees were in bloom and everything seemed fresh. As well as the spring, there was extra buoyancy in the air. The town suddenly appeared to be full of soldiers. They took over all the vacant houses. The school was partially closed again. They took over what was our cookery department. That was ok, every Friday the cooks would bake a load of currant buns, and the children would queue up to get their currant buns what a treat it was for them.

One Saturday evening, Agnes and Lil came around with their children. Elsie and I would have baby sit. It was quite usual for them all to stay overnight with us while they went out for a drink. The children were all in bed, playing around and singing their heads off. Elsie had gone out to meet mum. She suddenly dashed in, and said *"quick tidy up, put a clean cloth on the table, put the kettle on, and make the table look nice. Mum has invited some soldiers home for a cup of tea, and one is very posh"*. Well, what a laugh that was, in they all came, sat around the table. The posh one was telling them about his parents, and how that had to put their cars away, and they only had the pony and trap in which to travel in. The soldiers called him *'Uncle Cos'*: The other soldiers kept egging him on. I'm sure; they just liked to listen to him talking in this very posh voice. We all spent a happy jolly evening. Some one remarked to mum that it was a bit risky inviting strangers into the house, to which mum's reply was. *"Wherever my boys are, I hope someone has invited them into their homes, and made them feel welcome; that's the least we can do, also these young men may all be dead soon."*

You could feel the atmosphere in the air, that something big was about to happen. If it was, it had nothing to do with both Agnes and Olive being pregnant. One morning, at the end of May 1944, the whole town seemed too quiet. It seemed that overnight, the soldiers had all disappeared. The houses and the buildings that they had occupied stood empty and desolate. There also seemed a bit of a blackout, as far as the news was concerned. Someone, had taken a walk along the seafront, they came back amazed at the number of ships that were at anchor along the river. It was a big Armada of ships. *(Years later, I was to discover that my future husband John, who was a local boy, and was in the Royal Navy, was in one of those ships. He said how awful it was to see your hometown, and not being able to see his family, maybe for the last time. Like thousands of other young men he was just a month of his twentieth birthday).*

These young men who were all part of the liberation army, had been in many battles since the war started, but this one, was going to be the most horrendous battle of their lives.

The next day the ships had all gone. Instead the sky, at times was black with aircraft flying overhead. Then they gave out over the radio, that *D-Day* had arrived and that our troops had landed back in France. It was the 6th June 1944. It made mum glad that for one evening she had invited these young men into her home for a *'cup of tea'*. The news as you can imagine was very limited. The whole country seemed a bit subdued waiting for news.

That didn't last too long in our house, on the 11th of June, Agnes came in early one morning and wanted to see mum on her own. Suddenly, mum came in, and said to me, *"Agnes isn't very well, you will have to go and do her job for her until she's better"*. That didn't go down too well to say the least, and I refused to go, saying, *"Let the woman do her own work"!* After being promptly shoved out of the front door, mum said, that Agnes needed that job when she felt better and I was to go. . A couple of hours later, on arriving back home, mum told me to go upstairs to see Agnes who was in bed. There she was, with this bundle wrapped in her arms. I couldn't understand that the baby had arrived so quickly. I thought child labour lasted for hours not just one. That's how young girls were treated in those days, being brought up completely innocent of worldly things. So that's when Gwynneth was born, in the front bedroom in Wenham Drive, she was a lovely baby. She was the first one in the family for six years, and the first wartime baby. Len had brought home some lovely baby clothes, things we had never seen before. Little white sleeping suits trimmed with lemon, booties, matinee coats in beautiful soft wool, and a few other bits for the baby. Olive hadn't had her baby yet, but Len had brought the same home for her. The two best dressed babies in town.

The liberation of Europe seemed to be going well, although the casualties were horrendous. In the meantime we too, had a new menace in the sky, *the V-2 rocket*. They were more lethal than the *V-1*. They too, looked like a small plane as they soared overhead, with this jet of fire bursting out from the rear. The boys were home pretty frequently. Jack at this time was on his brother's sister ship, the *'Queen Elizabeth'*. The neighbours would ask mum if the boys were home, *"yes"* she would reply, *"have you seen them?" "No, but we heard Nell screaming."* I got told off for disturbing the neighbours. *"How would you like it?"* I replied, *"Having a wet flannel rubbed into your face or cold water poured into your ears first thing in the morning"*, to which, there was no reply, Jack was home.

Dad wasn't home as frequently as the boy's. He sailed on far slower ships, and his journeys were in different places. And so life went on in the nineteen forties. If Elsie had a Saturday morning off, she would have to help mum with the housework, whilst I had to go into Southend and queue up for the rations. First it was into *'Garons'* the Grocers just by the bridge, that's where we were registered to get our food, then down to *'Lyons tea shop,'* by *'Marks and Spencers'*, in the hope of getting some bread and four cakes. Home again to deposit the shopping, then over to the butchers to get our meat ration, vegetables from the greengrocer then the rest of the day was ours. All this too-ing and fro-ing and queing, would take up to about five hours of your day.

In the November, Jim asked mum if I could go and stay with Olive while he was at work, in case she needed anything. I was to sleep in Olive's bed with her. On getting into bed, she said, *"come on, couch up!"* Suddenly I felt this bump in my back. "What's that"? I said, *"It's only the baby kicking you"* she said, *'I don't like that,'* I replied, *"tomorrow I will go in with the girls"*. . I didn't mind taking the children to school, getting any shopping in from the village shops, but when she asked me to bring some mushrooms in for Jim's breakfast; I did shy away from that. There were only a couple of shops in the village, and when I asked her what shop to get them in, she burst out laughing. *"You don't "*, she said, *"You pick them up in the field when you take the children to school"*. Well, me being a townie, I didn't know one mushroom from another. *"Pam will show you"*, she said. I felt a right idiot, with a little nine year old telling me what to look for. *"We look for where the cows have been auntie"*, she said, *"That's where the best ones come from"*. Well that put me off mushrooms for life.

As well as Jim making dresses for them, every Friday evening, he would wash their hair in rainwater that came from the water butt outside. Their hair used to be lovely and soft. When I remarked about it to mum she said that rainwater was the best thing out for washing the hair. When he offered to do mine, I declined. Olive went into hospital, and I had to take the girls over to their Granma's in Benfleet, with strict instructions from Olive, that I was to take their rations over every week, and to make sure I saw them twice a week. For the two weeks that Olive was in the hospital, I only managed to see them once. Olive came home with her new baby son, Colin. I went over to fetch the girls. As she hadn't seen them for two weeks, she wanted to take them shopping, before they went back to the country. What a pantomime that turned out to be. We all trooped down to the bus stop, mum holding the baby. Olive with the two girls, and me. We get on the bus and away we went to Southend, Olive chatting away to the girls about what they had been doing etc. As she gets off the bus, she puts the baby all wrapped up in this lovely shawl that his uncle Len had brought home, straight into my arms. With the girls holding her hands, off they go skipping down the high street. As I stepped off the bus with baby Colin in my arms, you can imagine the horror of the people passing by, especially from a group of soldiers who had stopped and looked at me with their mouths open, just as though I had suddenly grown two heads. Mum took one look at their faces and remarked loudly, *"it's alright, you needn't look like that, and it isn't hers"*. She dashed after Olive and told her she would have to carry the baby, I was getting to many dirty looks. She just grinned, and said alright, *"I'll just keep in front of you"*, poor mum never got over that. She probably was worried in case people thought that her youngest daughter was a fallen woman. Young girls through the ages have been having babies. That was ok as long as they kept it hidden. So to see me stepping of a bus with this bundle in my arms was flaunting the rules. No wonder I got such dirty looks.

    Nineteen forty four was drawing to a close, it was

our 5th year of war and I think everyone was getting a bit tired, but at least the rockets had stopped coming over. The allies had ceased the rocket bases, and things were going well in Europe.

I decided that I needed to get a job; otherwise I was going to become a general dogsbody. The first job I had was in a general store. They sold everything from newspapers to food. At least I would be able to get some of what was kept under the counter. That didn't last long, I felt the old boy was getting a bit fresh, so I left, before I punched him one. I had three more jobs, one of which only lasted two hours, it was so boring, I eventually went to work at *The Echo Works*, where for the next five years, and I had one of the best times of my life.

Early in 1945, Olive and Jim decided to start a little business. The farm workers pay was still very small, they were very lucky, as the war appeared to be drawing to a close, people had started to move back into town, and property was becoming difficult to find. They managed to find a shop with living accommodation, in Milton Street. Jim stayed on in his job, and in the early hours of the mornings he would cycle every day to Stambridge. Olive, meanwhile, came to see mum, and down came the money pot. With five pounds from the pot, and leaving the children with mum Olive went off to the market. She brought as many as she could carry of baby chicks, she'd carried them on the bus, all the way from the market back to the shop, where mum was waiting for her with the children. She put these baby chicks into the shop window, and the next day she'd sold them all, and had to go back to the market and buy more; the business had started. On his way home from work, Jim would stop off at the mill to buy sacks of chicken feed. He'd carry it home on the handlebars of his bicycle. Len said that when he was home from sea, he would go on his bike and help him. As the business grew Jim gave up his job and the corn chandlers started to deliver the feed, until Jim managed to get a little van and pass his driving test. Then there seemed to be no stopping them, in the end they had three shops on the go, but they both had worked very hard to get that success.

Chapter Five

After the War

On May the 8th 1945, the war in Europe was over, what a great day that was, everybody seemed to be making for the High street and the sea front, it appeared that everyone wanted to be together to celebrate this wonderful day. On the 2nd of September 1945, the war in the Far East came to an end, after the Americans had dropped two atom bombs on Hiroshima and Nagasaki. The devastation these two bombs caused was horrendous and people felt every sympathy for the poor victims that was of course, until they saw the state that our own prisoners of war were in when they were released. Very similar to those poor people who were released from the concentration camps in Germany a few months previously. When the people saw them on the newsreels, they came out of the cinemas sobbing.

But now it was all over, thank god and all the boys would be coming home. All over the land, neighbours were already getting together to organise street parties. Streets were closed, tables and chairs were borrowed from everywhere, and they were all placed down the centre of the street, with sheets off the beds for tablecloths. Everyone contributed whatever they could so as to make this a monumental day, and they certainly did that. In the evening, some people brought out their pianos or their gramophones to play their records, so they could have a good old sing -song, and a 'knees – up'. They managed to get a few drinks, much of it home made wine, and beer, which, proved to be pretty potent, and a lovely time was had by all.

Of course that wasn't to be the end of the parties for a while. As the men came home it seemed as though every household had a *'bit of a do'* going. It really was a wonderful atmosphere. Unfortunately we don't get such feelings of camaraderie today.

As the war ended so families would once again be reunited. Len took me up to Wales to visit auntie Cissie and Uncle Jack. It was a lovely visit; Uncle Jack took us to Cardiff and showed us around. In the September, they came to visit us; Auntie Cissie brought her niece Frances, who was the same age as Elsie. Elsie remembers them taking her to Romford market on her twenty first birthday, and there they bought each of us a dress. I can remember the dresses each being of a different colour, red, blue and a green one and they had white polka dots on them. I can remember auntie Cissie sitting all afternoon taking the hem up on mine, because the dress was too long. The three of us were going to a dance that night and wanted to wear these dresses.

There were several visits from relations, cousins from Cornwall and Wales. Dad's brother uncle Charlie came down. Later on, Len would be taking his then future wife Margaret to meet Granma. During the years 1945 to 1950, Ted also had a visitor from Wales, his brother and his family came to stay with him, and his sisters went to stay with his sister Lil.

The men started to be discharged from the forces, the older ones first. Ted by this time was 46, so he was one of the first. On being discharged from the forces each serviceman was issued with what was termed as; *'The full Monty'*. It consisted of, one suit, one overcoat, one hat, shirt, underwear, socks, and shoes, and one suitcase. All this came from the London tailors *'Montigue Burton'*, hence the expression *"The Full Monty"*.

Dad who was fifty-six was still at sea. Elsie's boyfriend Eric was home and Elsie went up to

Worcester to meet him. When they arrived back to our house Elsie told mum that they wanted to get married in the May of 1946. So arrangements had to be put into motion. Dad still being at sea was unable to give her away, so Len said he would be home again by then and he would stand in for dad. So down once again came the money pot. They booked the wedding reception at *'Sam Issacs'*, who arranged the wedding cake as well, *(things were still very hard to get.)* Len brought her wedding dress home from New York, and it was absolutely gorgeous, as well as bottles of champagne and six champagne glasses, *(the wedding dress and the champagne glasses would be used later on by three more brides in the family.)*

The bridesmaids were Eric's cousin Margaret, and me. We were dressed in a very pale shade of lime green with very pretty little hats to match, and white gloves. We carried fresh spring flowers with trailing fern, and the two little ones were Pat and Rene, who had both just turned eight years of age. They would be dressed in pretty pale pink dresses, with a headband in the same material but edged with lace. They had white gloves and they carried little posies of spring flowers. The bride had on this gorgeous dress, on her head she had a little coronet of flowers with a long veil flowing down her back. She carried a bouquet of pink carnations. Both the little ones were so proud, as you can imagine two little girls to be. All dressed up in their long dresses, with flowers in their hair and carrying a posy of flowers. They were going to carry their Auntie Elsie's train all the way down the aisle of *St Mary's Church* Prittlewell. It was a very pretty wedding, the first in the family for ten years, the last being when Olive and Jim got married.

Before everyone set of for the church, David caused a bit of a stir. Len had taken him into town, and rigged him out in his first grown up clothes. A couple of pair of long trousers, new shoes and shirts, all ready for the wedding. He really looked great, whether it was because he had his long pants on and felt grown up, I don't know, but he started to strut as young boys are prone to do, that he asked, where his buttonhole was for the wedding. Because things were so expensive, they had forgotton the children. When he was told there weren't any. His reply was, *"well I'll find something'*; he wasn't going without his buttonhole. Some one remembered that we had loads of Lily-of-the-Valley growing in the front garden, so he and the other children had them that kept him happy. If you look at Elsie's wedding group photo, just behind his cousins you will see David in his first long pants, with the leaf of his Lily-of-the- Valley buttonhole stretched around his neck. His sister Phyllis looks as though hers is tickling her, but everyone has such a happy look on their faces.

The children, wouldn't be going to the reception either, it was too expensive. The reception with the cake had already cost Fifty Pounds, which in those days worked out at one mans wages for ten weeks. Margaret at thirteen, and Phyllis eleven, were in charge of the other five. Margaret had been given enough money to buy them all fish and chips, so they were quite happy. The brides party arrived back home, and then the real party began.

After the wedding Elsie and Eric went back to Worcester to live with Eric's parents, but every few weeks she would be home for a visit. When dad finally arrived back, he brought Elsie a pretty Opal ring, and some dress material for mum, when she asked him, *"What that was for?"* he replied, *"I thought you could make a dress for yourself".* She promptly told him what he could do with it; it was so garish it was to loud even for cushion covers.

The war had been over less than a year, and instead of getting better it was worse. With the devastation of the land caused by the war, it meant that approximately one quarter of the world was feeding the other three quarters. Our rations were cut once again; bread and oats had been rationed since 1946 and wouldn't be de rationed until 1948. By the end of 1946, Margaret left school and was the first of Agnes children to go out to work.

Early in 1947 dad was away again. I think this was probably his last time at sea, he was fiftyeight years of age, and had been going to sea off and on for the past forty-three years. But Jack was home, and didn't we know it. Margaret and her friends would go roller skating as often as they could to the Gliderdrome, which was situated along the sea front, by the gas works. This particular evening she came round and asked me if I would go with her, and could she stay the night, Mum said that was alright as long as her parents knew and that I looked after her.

I couldn't skate, but with a bit of encouragement from Margaret, I donned these skates. After struggling around the once, I gave it up as a bad job, and sat it out. They had a little coffee bar there and after a while Margaret who was a very good skater came over and asked to go and get a couple of coffees. Well, that was a laugh, have you ever seen any slap stick comedy. Well that's what it was like, she'd forgotten to tell me it was down a slope, I still had these skates on, and so off I went to the coffee bar. All I can say is that it's a good job the bar was placed at the bottom of this slope; otherwise I would still be going. I got the coffee, and then had to think about how I was going to get back to the top. One foot on the slope and I was back two, still I persevered but after a couple of other tries, I decided that the only way I was going to get back up that slope was to take off the skates. If they got nicked well so be it, at this point Margaret stood at the top of the slope laughing her head off. We very often had a laugh over that little episode.

Margaret had taken a shine to this boy, who was there with his mates. They offered to walk back home with us, and we had a very pleasant time walking along the beach. Perhaps, they thought they had to behave themselves as she had her old Auntie with her. The oldest of them was only about sixteen, the youngest fourteen, and me being seventeen there was no danger. They finally left us at the junction of London road and Hamlet court road; they had to make their way back to Thorpe Bay. We then walked home discussing the evening's events; up the road waving his arms about was Brother Jack. On reaching us, he did no more than clip Margaret around the ear and started kicking me down the road. All the while demanding to know where we had been and what had we been up to. Poor Margaret said to him, *"I'm going to tell my mum about you."* *"I don't care who you tell, you are not coming home this time of night"*. It was eleven o-clock and we had permission from mum to stay out till then.

Well, as far as I was concerned he wasn't going to get away with it. Mum told him off for hitting Margaret. I had my own revenge, we hadn't spoken since the incident, but two days later I had the most wonderful opportunity that I couldn't resist. I was coming down the stairs, and at that moment, the top of Jacks head was there right under my fist, so I thumped him one. *"Take that you spiteful thing"*, well he did stagger, which gave me the time to rush back up the stairs and lock myself in the bathroom, and there I stayed till he'd gone out, despite him trying to break the door down. Nothing more was said about it and we were soon friends again.

By the middle of 1947, Elsie was back at home again with the great news she was pregnant, and the baby was due in October and she wanted to come home to have it. All this was before the NHS was available, so she would have to pay for both the midwife and for the doctor if he was needed. The NHS wouldn't be implemented until the following year 1948. So, Elsie came back home in time to have her baby, a little boy Trevor. He was a lovely baby, and quite big. Elsie said that dad was home when he was born. He came in to see the new baby, picked him up and took him to the window and holding back the curtains said to his new grandson, *"can you see all those boys playing football, you'll be out there soon."*

Nineteen forty-seven was also the coldest year on record. The snow was so high it reached the top of our front gate, wherever you looked, were huge icicles, pipes that had burst, would have thick casings of ice on them. There was hardly any traffic on the roads as they were covered in thick Ice.

The emancipation of women started way back in the 1920's with the suffragette movement, but I believe it came to its full fruition at the end of the war. This would set the pattern for other young women.

The teenagers, who were just children when the war started six years, previously, were now emerging as young women. They had been mostly brought up in a matriarchal environment and now that the men were home couldn't understand why we had to defer to them for permission to do things. Everybody was equal and I for one wasn't having any of it. My three elder sisters were brought up to be a bit wary of dad, it was a different time. They had to be in by nine o-clock, and what he said went, and that was the end of it. Well, poor dad he didn't know what was coming with his youngest daughter.

This particular evening, I had mum's permission to go to a friend's house in the next road to play cards. She said that was all right, as she knew the family. After I told her what time I would be in, as it would be late, she replied that was all right, as well. So off I went. On my return home, there was poor mum practically wringing her hands. I wasn't late, she said, but your father has been carrying on about where you were, and what were you doing. *"Oh, has he, where is he"?* *"In bed"*, she replied, *"don't you go up there, you just go to bed quietly and he would have forgotten all about it in the morning".* I wasn't having any of that. I went into his bedroom, and woke him up, and told him,*" I've just come in, and what the time was, and for that for his information, I would be out late the following night as well. Mum knows all about it, and she said that it was ok, and that it had nothing to do with him, as long as my mother knew."* *"That's alright my dearr"*, he said, *"as long as your mother knows."*

Poor mum's face, as I came down the stairs looking agape. The next day, both my elder sisters had heard about it, and came round to make sure I was all right. Their faces were a picture. Poor Agnes had the habit if she was nervous of gently wringing her hands, and there she stood with her hands wringing, *"what did you say what did he do?"* *"Nothing"*, mum said, *"he just told her it was alright as long as I knew where she was". , "You young ones, you get away with murder if that had been any of us there would be all hell to pay."* Poor Agnes had to sit down until she got over it. Then Olive turned up, she'd told Jim to look after the shop as I was in trouble, and she had to make sure, I was all right. Down the road she came on her *'sitting up in bed'* bike. Mum, then repeated the tale, in all its detail. I couldn't understand their reaction, all their young lives they had been nervous of dad and he just turned out to be a big pussy cat,

Now that dad was home permanent, if young David wanted to go to the football match on a Saturday afternoon, he came round for his *'Pops'* and off they would go. The football stadium was situated in Grainger road, off the Sutton road back then, so it was quite a way to go for a small lad. If the boys were playing football in the street dad would join them, sometimes he was just a big kid himself,

The funniest bit about David, and his granddad which everyone thought was hilarious, was on a Sunday afternoon, David would come in, followed by his little sister Rene and their three Dolan cousins. Sometimes there would seem more than that, and say to his Nan, *"is Pops coming out"?* There would be poor old dad sitting by the fire on a Sunday afternoon with his hands folded nicely across his ample stomach, having his after dinner siesta. *"You'd better ask him",* she'd replied. *"Pops are you coming out?"* said David shaking his granddad *"Are you coming out"?* Poor old dad would gradually wake up, and looking at all the children, would say, *"Alright have you all got your money?"* Looking at mum, he then said, *"Give us a couple of bob Amy and a little extra for ice cream".*

Off they would all go like the *'Pied Piper of Hamlyn'*. Someone saw them all once, and reported back to mum what used to happen, and it went like this. "Getting on the bus, the children would all troop up the stairs playing merry hell and jumping around. The bus conductor would shout at them to 'sit down', leaving Dad to finish his sleep down below. Getting off the bus, they all trouped down to *'Garons Cinema'* where it was only nine pence to get in. Once inside, the kids would all go down the front and start playing around the seats, running up and down the aisle, whilst dad would be fast asleep in the back row.' Off they would all troop back home and it would all be repeated the following week.

When Olives little boy Colin came down, dad would play with him showing him magical tricks; pulling coins from behind Colin's ear, making him guess which hand the penny was in, making funny shapes with handkerchiefs, and anything else that would amuse a three to four year old.

Elsie would be down more often, now she had Trevor. She used to say he was a bit restricted where he could play, in Eric's mother's house. Down here, he had more space. Whenever Phyllis' illness flared up, she would often go and stay with Elsie in Worcester. Elsie was glad of her company; I think she felt a bit lonely up there especially coming from a big family.

Dad had managed to get himself a little job as a night watchman. He was already approaching sixty years of age. I don't recall exactly where he used to work. Late one night, mum, was woken up by the police, who told her that dad was in hospital with head injuries. He wasn't too badly injured, but needed a few stitches. Apparently he had witnessed a robbery, and had got hit on the head for his efforts. He was off work for a couple of days but soon went back again. He had found a bag containing some *'booty'* including some jewellery. He handed it in to the police and was told, if it was not claimed within 6 months it was his. When dad went back in 6months, it had already been claimed, so poor dad was out of luck again!

This was the year 1949 when both Len and Jack would be married; Len to Peggy Rose Carr, and Jack, to Ann Amelia Wingfield. Len and Peggy would be the first two getting married in the March. Peggy would be wearing the same dress as Elsie had worn at her wedding, and I was to be her bridesmaid. Len had their three tier wedding cake, made on board the ship. The wedding went off very well, everybody happy and loads of pictures taken outside St. Mary's Church Prittlewell. Their wedding reception was held in the Bungalow Tea Rooms, which, was opposite Priory Park gates.

I don't remember anything about the wedding reception, which I, thought was rather sad, due to my trusting my dear brother Jack. It was a very cold day, and I didn't have a coat on. As I went into the hall, Jack said *"here"*, handing me a bottle. *"Have a good swig of this"*. Well I did, and being as I had never drank any spirits at all, it went straight to my head. The next thing is mums' standing beside me saying, *"What are you two up to?" "Nothing"*, he said, *"I'm just giving her a drink to warm her up"*. *"By the looks of her,"* she said, *"I think you had better take her home before she shows us all up."*

So just as I was, my dear brother Jack takes me down to the bus stop and promptly sits me down on the trolley bus. Paying the fare, he tells the conductor to drop me off two stops away. There I sat, in a thin bridesmaid's dress, flowers in my hair and still carrying my bouquet. The conductor drops me off at the boom of Wenham Drive. Like some homing pigeon, I headed for home. Pulled the key out by its string and went inside. That's all I remember. Apparently, as he'd got back to the hall pretty quickly, mum sent him after me to make sure I was alright. I don't remember who was with him, but after searching the house and looking everywhere finally found me hanging over our old wooden mangle in the garden. I must have walked straight through the house, until the mangle stopped me going any further. Anyway he did put me to bed, still fully clothed with the flowers still in my hair. Would anyone like a brother? Ha! Ha! Ha! I was going out, to the kursaal that night dancing, when my friends came to fetch me. I heard mum say, *"she can't go out, she's ill,"* but I shouted down from my bedroom, *"no I'm not, and I'm going dancing",* which I did.

Jack and Anne's wedding was next, out came the lovely dress again. I think Ann had six bridesmaids, of which I was one. That too, was a lovely wedding, and their reception was held in the Railway Hotel. I can remember that one quite well, because that is where I was able to introduce my boy friend to the family. I told mum that I was meeting him down in the bar, and she could come and meet him if she wanted to, which she did. Then, one by one, the rest of the family came down, both my brothers came down to give him the once over. Jack and his new wife knew him anyway, as he was a local boy. We were to get married two years later and our wedding reception would be held in the same hall, I also wore the same dress and we used the same champagne glasses, two of which I still have.

In 1948-49, Dior had designed the *'New Look'*. After the starkness of the war years, it was lovely to see different clothes appearing in the shops. The suits consisted of a long slim fitting skirt with a slit up each side and a little jacket that fitted into the waist, with a flounce at the back, little buttons that did up to the neck. With that, you wore high heeled, stiletto shoes with ankle straps. They looked lovely and it felt good to have something smart to wear. The only problem was you had to take small steps, no more striding along like you were used to. With the high heeled, shoes on, you had to learn to walk again, *like a lady*, whatever that is. Of course that wasn't the only problem, you couldn't jump on a bus like you used to. If you wanted to do that, you would have to hitch the skirt up around your thighs. You had to step sideways on to the bus, as though your knees were tied together.

It was now the 1950s; there would be three more

babies in the family. Olive would be having her baby in the April, Ann and Jack would be having their first child in September, and Agnes would be having hers in the October. Olive decided to have her baby at mums, as with all the other babies, out would come, the 'brass kettle'. The brass kettle was given to dad by Grandma. Apparently it has always been handed down to the eldest son, at that moment it belonged to dad. This kettle was always used in the family for home confinements. The last time it was used was for Elsie, now it was coming out again for Olive. Little Jennifer was born on the 2nd of April 1950, like all babies she was lovely. Unlike her cousin Gwyneth, who was born in the upstairs front bedroom, Jenny was born in the front living room, the same as her cousin Trevor. Olive said it would make it easier for mum to look after them. Jim would come down every evening after closing the shop. After a week, he asked her to go back home, so arrangements had to be made with the midwife to do her daily visits to the shop. She was none too pleased about, it but mum promised to go up every day, while Olive needed her, which she did.

Ann's baby was also born at home in September 1950, in their flat in Carlingford Drive. I took my two weeks annual leave to take care of them. Naturally, they were both thrilled to bits to have a little boy, Phillip. The story told is, how Jack coming home from work one day, heard some children making a lot of noise. He went out after them, and told them if they didn't be quite he would send his boy out after them. Poor little scrap, only a couple of days old, and already his father is setting him up for a scrap.

Agnes' little girl Glynis, was born on the 16th of October 1950. With Glynis' birth complication's had arisen, and Agnes had to be admitted to hospital. The Doctor and the midwife had both been with her, but she needed to be hospitalised, the doctor told Ted that when he got back from the hospital he was to go and see him as he wanted to know what the outcome was. When Ted came back from the hospital he called in to mum before going to see the doctor and told us that it was a little girl and that she had loads of black curly hair,

Now that the three babies had arrived, it was time for me to get ready for my own wedding.

John Edward Parsons and I were married on the 13th of January 1951, in St Mary's Church Prittlewell; in the same dress and in the same church as my sister and my brothers before me. My bridesmaids were my niece's Margaret, Pamela, and little Gwyneth. Our reception was also going to be in the Railway Hotel. The only difference was this time it was my father who was giving me away, I believe I was the only one of his daughters he gave away.

That was a very busy day for me. We were up at the reception hall laying and setting all the tables and chairs out. Johns' mother and his sister, who lived just around the corner, came to help. Everybody then had to leave to get ready for church. I was getting married at half past two, and I had to wash my own hair, no money to spare for hairdressers back then. About eight, of John's shipmates came, that were in the band with him, but they were a bit late, the service had already started and there was this loud banging on the church door shouting to be let in. Anyone would have thought it was some irate father forbidding his daughters' marriage, but my father was standing beside me. My niece's had a wonderful time when we came out of the church; the sailors were chasing them all round the tombstones.

As John was still in the Royal Navy, he could only get a forty eight hour pass, and had to be back in the barracks, at five o/clock on the Monday morning so of course no honeymoon. We were having a war in Korea at the time, so he had another eighteen months put on his service, hence the forty-eight hour pass. We never knew if suddenly he would have sailed away to the war zone.

Everyone had now left home and leading their own lives. I went back to work and life went on the same, still queuing up. Still trying to *'make do and mend'*, and still trying to keep warm in this cold winter. Although, we did have one concession, we were able to buy fur lined, boots with nice thick soles. It made a big difference not having to stand at the bus stops in paper thinned soles. I still lived at home in two rooms whilst John was in Chatham Barracks

Mum and dad's lives went along quietly, still going out with Agnes and Ted on a Saturday, Elsie and Eric were down quite frequently. One time she came home and made mum and dad laugh over young Trevor, apparently she had him on the bus one day taking him shopping, when suddenly at the top of his little voice to the tune of, *"Glory, Glory Hallelujah"*, started to sing, *"does the driver want to wee, wee does the driver want to wee, wee does the driver want to wee, wee, well the girls in the back seat does"*. Mum said it reminded her of Olives little girl Pam, when she was small. One of the popular songs when Pam was tiny was, *"Horsey hold your tale up, hold your tail up, keep the sun out of my eyes"*. She would skip down the road singing her head off, that was ok, until she saw a horse doing its business, then she would add, *"O look mummy, large lumps!, large lumps!,"* They didn't know where to put their red faces. Nearly as bad as her auntie Agnes when she was a toddler, if she saw two dogs in the street making babies she would shout out, *"O look Mummy those doggies are playing a knees up Neddy and a bow, wow, wow "*. Out of the mouths of babes!

That August during carnival week, the Royal Naval Band came over to play in the procession. On a Wednesday afternoon, I was still at work although arrived home a little earlier than usual. As I came in the front door mum said, *"Johnny's home, asleep on your settee, but I haven't woke him up, I'll leave it to you, the kettle is on"*, I peeped around the door, and saw this 'Matelot' fast asleep with his back to me. *"Right, I'll make a pot of tea and wake him up"*, but I had this little niggle in my head, and thought I would go back and have another look. It wasn't John; it was some stranger fast asleep on my settee in my room. So I searched the rest of the house looking for my missing husband, couldn't find him anywhere. When I told mum she said, *"Who is he?" "I don't know"*, I replied, *"I have never seen him before"*. That got us both wondering how he'd got in. Anyway, I made the tea and woke this sailor up. *"O, hi Nell"*, he said, *"Hope you don't mind, John said it would be alright. "How did you get in"*, I asked. *"O John said if the front door is locked, try around the back and I will be with you shortly, so I did and got in through the back window."* I was furious, *"so where is he?" "O, I left him and the rest boys asleep under the Pier"!*

Well, he got the rest of the Pier when he did eventually arrive back home. Just in time to have a good telling off. *"What do you think this is a doss house?" "I'm sorry, I thought you wouldn't mind". "Good job, it wasn't night time"*, I replied, *"I may well have got into bed with a strange sailor!"* After a cup of tea, and something to eat, they all, had to head back to the sea front, to catch their special coach back to the barracks.

They would all come over, sometimes for a weekend, and sleep on the floor in our living room. If it got a bit chilly at night they would snuggle down under the carpet. My sister Agnes, and her sister in law Lil would take great delight in coming over early in the morning, to wake them all up with a cup of tea, and run the vacuum cleaner over them, to get the carpet fluff off of their uniforms.

In the September of 1951, little Trevor was admitted to hospital. He was very poorly, and they diagnosed T. B, Meningitis. Poor baby, he had to spend his fourth birthday in hospital. He seemed to recover in the November, and Elsie took him home. They had just been allocated their own home, and were waiting to move in when poor little Trevor had a relapse on the first of January 1952. In the meantime I was pregnant and my baby was due in March. Mum was with Elsie in Worcester giving her as much support as she could, through this terrible time. In the meantime, at the end of January, I had developed Eclampsia. The same complaint that had killed my sister Winnie, so I was admitted to hospital, Trevor was still very ill and things didn't look too good for him. Because at the time I was critically ill, they decided that the baby would have to be delivered. On the 9th of February 1952, my daughter Maureen Alexandra was born, weighing only four and a half pounds. Poor John, he couldn't get home all during this crisis. Eventually, he went to his commanding officer for permission to have leave of absence, which he granted verbally and told him to be on his way and he would send a telegram confirming his permission. Poor John, he had only been home for twenty- four hours and the police came and arrested him for being '*A W O L*'. They took him back to Chatham under guard and locked him in the cells. After a few more hours had passed, they discovered the telegram still sitting in the communications office, and they then allowed him his leave, but only for twenty- four hours.

While the entire crisis was going on at this end,

unfortunately up in Worcester, Trevor was loosing his battle for life and sadly he passed away on the 20th of February 1952. Back down here my baby was twelve days old, and was still struggling for hers in the special care baby unit at Rochford. I wasn't allowed even to hold or touch her till she was about a month old. When she was six weeks old and weighing just five pounds, I was allowed to bring her home. Following Trevor's funeral, Elsie and Eric had returned home with mum. As I walked through the door, Elsie was standing there waiting for us, I plonked my baby straight into her arms. I couldn't bear to think of the heartache my sister was going through. Eric and John went to have a drink to *'wet the baby's head'* and came back, pushing the pram. When my sister Agnes saw her, she said, *"O my god isn't she small, I would be too frightened to touch her."* All of her babies had been big eight to ten pounders.

And so time moved on, and we all went about our daily chores. Although everybody seemed to be working hard, things didn't seem to improve. Agnes was still working at her little job. Lil had just had another baby a little while before Maureen was born, it was a little girl, Linda. Agnes's baby Glynis, was only sixteen months older than Maureen, and when Agnes went to work, she would bring her around for mum and I to look after. So I would pop her into the pram with Maureen, and off we would go to feed the ducks in Priory Park, or for a walk down Hamlet Court Road. The same thing would happen when I went to Olives, which I frequently did. Sometimes she would ask me to give her a hand, as she had been so busy. I would do whatever she wanted me to. Otherwise, I would take Jenny, who was twenty -two months older than Maureen, she too would sit in the pram and off we would go. One day, Olive asked me to check on Jims' dinner. He would be in shortly and she hadn't had time to see to it. Off I went, then returned to her and said, *"Do you know what you have done, you've put his potatoes in the same pan as his cabbage?" "Yes, I know, just leave it, what the eye doesn't see, his heart wont grieve, anyhow it will all look the same when it's on the plate".* On one occasion Olive became a bit worried at me staying with her to help out. She asked mum, *"Does John moan at her because his dinner is not on the table when he arrives home from work?" "O no, no, no",* she said. *"She is not like you older girls, if she isn't in, he gets the tea for her!"*

John had come out of the Royal Navy in August 1952. This was going to be our first chance of married life. Instead of a two week pass here and there, and a week's leave now and again, things would be a bit different. John started back to work for the same firm he worked for as an apprentice before the war, they were steamfitters and heating engineers. As he started back to work mum would come out with all this old adage, probably the same things she would have said to my elder sisters, *" Have you got John's dinner on? A man likes his dinner on the table when he's finished a day's work. Even if it isn't ready, always lay the table up, and then he will wait because he knows something is on the way". Well I told her that we lived in another world now, and if his dinner wasn't ready, well tough".* That would get her in a fluster, she still treated men as though were the master and their wife's were slaves.

In 1952 David who was sixteen years of age, had been very ill in hospital for over 12 months was now home at last, as was his Uncle Len. Taking one look at David he asked Agnes and Ted if he could take David to sea with him for week. David was over the moon, it had always been his ambition to be able to go to sea like his grandfather and his uncles, but that sadly wasn't to be, so this week away with his uncle Len was extra special like a big adventure.

Len being a 'Chief Butcher' had his own cabin. Behind the cabin door was his bunk, underneath that were storage drawers. At the bottom of the bunk was the wardrobe, next to that was Lens desk. Along the wall underneath the porthole was a very large settee all covered in a lovely floral material, and there David was to sleep. The cabin was all done out in beautiful mahogany. The toilet facilities were on the wall opposite the bunk. As David woke up each morning he would look out of the porthole and see either the ship leaving harbour or entering one. He would rush up on deck to watch the seamen going about their jobs and then he would go down into the galley to join his uncle for breakfast.

The cook trying to build him up after his long illness would serve him up with six eggs, loads of bacon, sausages, and fresh bread just out of the oven. In the evening's, when the men went ashore, David would go as well. As they returned to the ship they would have to report to the duty policeman, David was always the first to shout out *"Windrush", "ok", he would reply, "Go ahead"*. I expect that memory, stayed with him for many a year.

About 1954, Agnes came over one day, and said that Phyllis was getting married, and that she, was going to have to do the reception, and would I help. *"Of course she will," mum pipes up. She loves cooking; she's always messing about in the kitchen."* It's a good job I loved baking isn't. So with the help of the only cookbook I possessed, which was a paper backed, '*Stork margarine* cookbook', that had been given away free. They expected me to produce a banquet and things still weren't all that plentiful. Also, in those days, you must remember that only rich people had fridges, and freezers were unheard of, so you had the added problem of keeping the food fresh. Two days before the wedding, with mum, Agnes and Lil all looking on, I started to bake cakes and sponges. Orange, and lemon, flavoured ones, with slices of crystallized fruit on the top. That was alright, till I saw Lil taking the slices off the top and eating them. Quiches were just about coming into fashion, they were known at that time as 'Italian flans', so I made some of them, as well as the usual things that people had at their weddings, at the time. I thoroughly enjoyed doing it all.

Throughout that period, between the fifties and sixties, lots of things would take place. Agnes' children would start getting married, and having babies and making both her and Ted grandparents. As would Olives' two elder girls, which were another two weddings I helped cater for. I also went with Olive to choose the wedding outfit that she was going to wear to Pam's wedding. It was a pretty pink tweedy looking suit with two skirts; one slim line, and the other one, was pleated. The complete ensemble, consisted of, new shoes with a handbag to match and a white blouse.

On the day of the wedding she came down and asked me if I would do her hair and put a bit of makeup on for her. *"Not too much, because Jim won't like it"*. I had never known my sister to wear any makeup, although she and Winnie did when they were both young. I did her hair, put just a little bit of face cream and powder on her and a little lipstick. *"How's that mum and dad?" she said. Mum said, "That's alright, and dad told her she looked lovely.* When Jim came in, she said, *"well what do I look like, very nice"*, he said, of course she preened, until he said, *"but you can take that off of you face, I don't like it"*. I was quick to jump in defence of my sister, *"well it isn't your face I told him, it's hers and she likes it"!!* . To her credit she did leave it on, and looking at the photo's now, after all these years she kept it on, and Jim must have liked it too because they are both looking happy and smiling.

All this set me back to thinking about my own wedding. Young Rene was just fourteen, and wore a black and white tweedie coat, with a black velvet collar, and a black Tam-a-Shanty. As she walked into the living room, everyone said, *"whoo, don't you look smart"*, but dad had to go one better and said, *"you look lovely just like a little French Tart"*. My quick reply to that was, *"and how do you know what a French Tart looks like? You had better watch him Mum"*, *"fancy talking to the child like that"*, she said. Poor dads, face he was only trying to compliment one of his granddaughters.

Also in that period more babies would be born. In 1954 Ann and Jack had a little baby girl, Valerie Anne. The next year my own second daughter was tragically born asleep. I had the same condition, as I had with Maureen, Eclampsia, and was once again very critically ill. I was not expected to recover; everyone was prepared for the worst. Phyllis baby son John was also born, making Agnes and Ted, grandparents for the first time. The next year on the 11thMay 1955, Len and Margaret's baby son Ian Christopher was born. The brides and babies seemed to be coming along at a fast rate. Agnes' next two girls, Margaret and Rene, Olive and Jim second daughter Pat, weddings, all followed by their babies,

Mum would send dad over to the post office to get their pensions. , One day she said to me, *"your father always seems short, when he brings it back, but he doesn't seem to have brought anything"*. The next week, she followed him over to the post office. There's dad, just coming out of the post office, Glynis and Maureen both holding his hands, plus a couple of

Maureen's little friends who lived up the road. The next port of call was the sweetie shop, in they all go, coming out clasping a bag of sweets each. She's waiting for him when he arrives home, handing over all the money, *"its short", he said, "what have you done with the rest," "I've brought the children a few sweets, surely you don't begrudge your grandchildren a few sweets",* "no I don't", she replied, *"but I'm not paying for half of the street!".* That was dad like the "Pied Piper of Hamlyn" where children were concerned.

Dad found himself a little job delivering pamphlets through peoples' front doors. He had a bit of an accident and had a fall and broke his ankle. Unfortunately that was the start of the slippery slope for dad. In 1958, dad suffered a stroke, poor mum had just got up to make their early morning tea, and there was a big thud. We all reached the bedroom together, and there was poor dad flat on the floor, paralysed all the way down his left side. John managed to pick him up from the floor and laid him back onto the bed. We then called the doctor who came down and confirmed what we had suspected, and he was hospitalised. When he was discharged from the hospital he was completely immobile.

Agnes in the meantime had moved from the flat in Gainsborough Drive to a larger house in Brighton Road. She changed her job and became a cook in a café and she loved it. The place where she had worked for a few years would be too far away, so I took that over, it was in Victoria Avenue as a domestic. Besides this, I also worked four days a week in the geriatric unit at Rochford hospital. Starting at one thirty in the afternoons until, ten o-clock at night, this included Saturdays. Before going to work, I would help mum make dad comfortable for the afternoon. This included washing, dressing and toileting. Then after arriving home, about ten thirty at night, I would start again to get him ready for bed and make him comfortable for the night. Despite both John and I working hard we didn't seem to be getting anywhere. We needed a change.

Before dad had his stroke, we had talked it over, and discussed it with both mum and dad about us upping sticks and emigrating, to Australia on the 'Ten pound Passage Scheme', *(Ten Pound Pom)*. Due to the considerable support and help that mum required with dad, we decided to put a hold on things for a while. We had already set the wheels in motion, obtaining all the literature, and books from the library, and had completed the application forms from Australia House which were accepted, but for now it was all on hold while we waited to see if dad would eventually become more mobile.

By the middle of 1959, Olive was pregnant and would be expecting her new baby early in the New Year. Jim and the rest of her children were all awaiting the happy event. Pat had married, and had a little baby boy Kevan, making Olive and Jim grandparents for the first time.

Olive and Jim's second son was born on the 4th February 1960. They had called in to show us their new son, on the way home from the hospital. He was a lovely big baby, and the image of Jim, everyone was so pleased, especially Jenny who at nearly ten years of age, was just the age to want to look after her baby brother.

A few weeks later tragedy was to strike. Mum received a phone call from one of Olive's girls, she was crying down the phone trying to tell her grandmother that her mother had gone. For a while poor mum couldn't understand what she was saying, *"gone where? Gone where?"* With that mum fell against the wall totally shocked, *"Olives' gone!"* she said and *"Jim is on his way over to get me"*, *"Olives family need me there"*. She then had to go and tell dad, there they were holding hands crying their eyes out. *"Why he kept saying, why, it should have been me, I have had my life, she's too young and with a young family she's needed here I'm not."*

Shortly after Jim arrived poor man, also understandably in complete shock, and asked mum to go back to Benfleet with him. Dad of course was completely immobile, so I had to stay with him. Mum stayed up there the rest of the day, and went back and forth, each day while Jim needed her. In turn of course mum needed to be with Olives' children.

Jim wanted Olive buried with her sister Winnie. Jim mentioned a strange thing to mum, he said the night before Olive died she'd had a sort of dream. She told him the next morning that, Winnie had been with her. She said, *"I hope they don't have to take me out of the window like they did her"*. I asked mum for an explanation of why she should say that. She went on to explain that when our sister Winnie died the doors were to small to bring her in, and to be able to take her out again, so they had to take a window out, and put it back after her funeral. So Olive was buried with her beloved sister in the family grave.

Two years later dad also died. Dad who had never had a cold in his life had developed Pneumonia. The doctor told mum there wasn't anything they could do just to keep him comfortable. It must have been their Celtic blood taking over. Like his daughter Olive before him, although he seemed to be unconscious, mum, Elsie and I heard him say, *"no, not yet girls, not yet"*. A little while after that, he opened his eyes, and said to mum, *"you'll be alright won't you Amy, you'll be all right, you've got the children"*. Don't you worry *about me"*, she said, *"I'll be alright, you just take care of yourself"*. Still holding hands, dad passed away on the 25th January 1962.

Dad was also buried in the family grave with his beloved daughters. It seemed that John and I would now be unable to go to Australia. Jack and Ann were going and it seemed that their arrangements were far in advance of ours. After dad had died, and with both John and I out to work all day, plus Maureen being at school, there was hardly anything for mum to do, so she would take herself of to see Agnes.

I can understand how she was feeling, after having a big family, and having dad to nurse for the last four years, she was lost. In Agnes' house she was once again in the midst of a busy family life. They both said that if John and I still wanted to emigrate then go ahead. Agnes and Ted were quite happy to have mum with them. Once again she felt needed. She was also able to resume the Saturday evening out; she'd been unable to go much with dad being ill.

Unfortunately things didn't go according to plan, despite many phone calls and trips to Australia house in London, our sailing tickets never came forward. Jack and Ann had received theirs and had a sailing date. Ours still failed to turn up. We had sold the house, all our furniture had gone, and we were staying with my niece Rene and her husband Vernon in Shoebury. School was about to start, Maureen's education would be interrupted if we didn't do something. We bought another house in Caulfield Road in Shoebury. Maureen then attended Caulfield Road School. I got myself another Job as a care assistant in Delaware House an old people's home working shift work. We then settled down tried to relax after the trauma. I can well remember the day we moved in, it was Nov: the 22nd 1962 the day that President Kennedy was assassinated.

As Christmas approached, mum would be coming to me for Christmas Day, as would Elsie and Eric. A few days before Christmas there was a ring at the doorbell. As I opened the door to my delight and surprise there stood two of Olives' children. I hadn't seen them since they had lost their mother. I told them that their Nan, aunt and uncle would be coming over for Christmas Day, and it would be lovely if they and their dad were able to be there as well. Jenny came back a couple of days later to say they would be coming, but unfortunately her dad would be working. So off she and Maureen went, shopping down Southend high street. We had a lovely Christmas Day together, and my niece Rene and her husband Vernon and the two little boys were able to join us for tea.

Chapter Six

Mum's Life without Dad

By the October of 1965 I with my little family was already living in Canada. On the 11th of December 1966, seventeen days, before mums seventy fifth birthday, she had her first holiday abroad and her first flight in a plane. She was coming over to Canada to stay with us for as long as she wished. We had bought her an open ticket, which lasted twelve months, in order that she could go back home at anytime. John, Maureen and I went up to Malton airport in Toronto to await the arrival of her plane, worrying all the seven and half hours journey time, if she would be alright. I needn't have worried a bit. As she stepped down from the plane, you would have thought that she was just stepping of the Southend bus, instead of a big 747 Boeing air jet. We were so proud of her, she thought the flight was wonderful, and she didn't feel a bit tired, and that everyone on the plane had been very kind, and so started mums stay with us in Canada.

She had a wonderful time; we often took her down to Niagara Falls on a Sunday afternoon. It was only about an hours' drive from where we lived, in Burlington, Ontario. One day she said that she would like to go over to America to see what it was like over there. We drove over the Niagara suspension bridge and arrived at immigration. We all had our passports, but what we had forgotten was a visa for mum. We were all right, and could cross anytime as we were residents living in Canada, so we didn't think about mum. Looking at all our passports, he took another look at mum and then again at her passport and asked her where she was born *"Wales"*, she replied. Looking a bit surprised, the Immigration Officer said, *"Wales where's that? I haven't heard of it, where is it"*. By this time we were all grinning, even the immigration officer who was smiling at her. *"Sorry honey"*, he said, *"I would let you in, but they may not allow you to come back in again. They aren't as nice as we are, and you wouldn't like it over there anyway. It isn't very nice; we are a lot nicer over here in Canada. You stay over here with us and enjoy your visit in this country"*. *"Thank you"*, she replied, *"I wasn't too fussed about going over anyway"*. Ever after she would tell people that, I tried to get into the United States once, but they would have me.

As it was Mothers day, we thought that we would try to get in touch with Jack and his family in Australia. So I phoned our local exchange and explained what I wanted which was a surprise phone call to her son Jack in Australia, in those days you could not make a direct call and Jack was not on the phone at that time., The operator got through to Vancouver, they in turn got in touch with the exchange in Elizabeth South Australia. Back came, all these voices', finally to me. He wasn't listed but would I like them to contact his nearest neighbour, to go and fetch him? *"Yes please!"* Back went all the voices to Australia, after about ten minutes Jack was on the phone, Calling Mum over, I said, *"there's someone here, who would like to speak to you,"* and handed her the phone. She couldn't get over it. *"Its Jack!"* she kept saying. That was the best Mother's Day present we could give her. I wasn't charged any money until she was actually speaking to Jack. What a wonderful service, for 'Bell Telephones'.

She had a wonderful time seeing all the sights of Toronto. Looking across Lake Ontario she could see the lights twinkling over in the States. We would take her out Sunday afternoons to the Indian Reserve, to let her see how they lived, watching a snow storm from the living room window, and many other things.

Agnes' was getting a bit worried. Because of the new development that was taking place in the town, it meant that Agnes and her family would have to be rehomed. She was getting a little bit concerned that if mum wasn't home she might not be included as part of Agnes family, that would be needing accommodation. Mum finally returned home in the middle of May 1967. The snow was just about to clear from the ground and the spring flowers were already peeping through. She'd had had a lovely holiday, and looked wonderful went she went back home after her big adventure.

By the end of 1974, I was back home from Canada. Once I had got myself settled, mum was able to spend time with me. When I arrived back home I can remember Agnes putting her arms around me, and saying, *"I'm so glad you are back, I haven't got to worry about Mum any more"*. Although she would go to Worcester to spend time with Elsie and her husband Eric, maybe she thought they might be too far away in case of any emergency, besides which mum was now eighty-three. Agnes' husband Ted was also in poor health, so one can understand Agnes' relief.

In 1978, mum was to have a stroke that shocked everyone. Poor Agnes she was heartbroken. I had never seen my sister cry before, but there she was, with her arms tightly around mum, holding her close crying, *"don't leave me mum, don't leave me"* . I told Agnes that she wasn't leaving anyone, and she was going to get back on her feet. Looking at mum, I said, *"don't think you are just going to lie there, you have got to get up on your feet"*. She was admitted to the hospital and, there, her rehabilitation started. The whole family took it in turns, and a rota was set up to make sure that two at a time would always be with her. David and Maureen did the night shift together, David couldn't make out how Maureen being so tiny was able to lift her Nan up the bed the way she did. Mum was so frightened, at eighty six this was only the second time she had been ill and admitted to hospital, the first being when she had her Gall bladder removed At Southend and was sent for recovery at the Victoria Hospital in Kings Road in the 50's.' *"I don't like it in here", she kept saying," I want to go home".* I promised her, that, if in three weeks time she could climb a few stairs, I would take her home. Mother of course, being very strong and determined, did climb a short set of stairs, and then I took her home with John me. Agnes' staircase was so very steep; she would never have managed to climb them. My daughter Maureen, who at that time was a Sister at St Thomas's hospital in London would come home whenever she could, and made sure that everything was as it should be with her grandmother, also that we were getting all the medical help that was needed.

It was now 1980, and mums eighty eighth birthday had arrived. Jack was home on holiday with his wife Ann, and so, a party was arranged. All of her remaining children were there, and as many of her grandchildren that could make it. She had a large birthday cake set out with two number eight numerals. The first birthday cake she'd had since she was a child. She was a bit overwhelmed to see so many of her family there especially, her son Jack and Ann, all they way from Australia. Little did we all realise that it would be the last time we would all be together.

In 1982 a further tragedy was to happen. Agnes who hadn't been very well for a while was admitted to hospital. Unfortunately Agnes never recovered from her illness and passed peacefully away on the 7th

February 1982. Her poor husband Ted and her children were naturally heartbroken. Mum didn't say too much, but at night when I could hear her crying, I would go and sit beside her on the bed. She had lost her beloved daughter, who all of Agnes life had never been too far apart, and had always been there for when ever they had needed each other. Sadly that wasn't to be the end of it. There was to be further heartbreak for Agnes' children. Their father, Ted who for many years had suffered from Emphysema, was taken ill, and passed away in the Nov of 1982. Mum was deeply upset and said,"*I have not only lost Agnes, now Ted has gone, and I have lost my two best friends*".

Six more years would pass along with regular visits from all of her grandchildren. Once or twice a year she would go up to Worcester to spend time with Elsie until she wanted to come home. As each year passed, mum was becoming more frail and immobile and unable to do things herself, other than feed herself. I then had to make one of the worst decisions of my life, what to do about mum. There wasn't too much room at my home and she needed more space in which to get around. She and I discussed the problem, and she agreed to go and have a look at the care home for the elderly, which was just around the corner from me. I put her in her wheelchair and off we went. It was a very nice place, and the added bonus was that her eldest granddaughter worked there, also it was run, by a friend of her granddaughter Maureen; they had been student nurses together. She had a lovely room that overlooked a little park where she could watch the children at play, her own television, and plenty of company if she wanted. I would pop around each lunch time and again in the evenings to sit with her and tell her all the family gossip. She loved to hear stories of what all her family were up to. Her grandchildren would go to see her, and kept in touch.

After a series of suspected heart attacks mum was admitted to hospital with Pneumonia on Christmas Eve of 1990. Two days after her 98th Birthday, mum passed peacefully away on New Years Eve, surrounded by as many of her family who could be there. All through their lives she had been there for them, and now, at the end of hers, they were there for her. Mum was buried with her beloved family, in the family grave.

All through mum and dads lives, as in all families, was to run tragedy and heartbreak, but also two others would run hand in hand as well; lots of love and laughter, and those last two, are the ones we should cling to.

Nos Da Cariad
God Bless
Sleep Well

Bibliography

Martin, Edward A. 1991. **The Martin Family of Stithians in Cornwall,** 4th Edition, W.A. Martin, Oak Tree Farm, Hitcham, Ipswich, Suffolk, IP7 7LS

Briggs, ASA. 1994, **A Social History of England, New Edition from the Ice Age to the Channel Tunnel, BCA,** London.

Opie, Robert, 1998, **The Wartime Scrapbook, from Blitz to Victory 1939-1945,** Cavendish Books London.

HMSO, 1993, Union **Jack, A Scrapbook, British Forces Newspapers 1939-1945,** The Imperial War Museum, Dept. of Printed Books, HMSO Publications, London.

Newnes, George, 'The Daily Mirror', 1964, Our **Finest Years, Foreword by Field Marshall the Viscount Montgomery of Alamein,** George Newnes Ltd, Southampton.

Worsdale, Jim. 2001, **A Southend Childhood,** MGA Printing Westcliff-on-sea.

Herbert, A. P. 1992, **The Battle of the Thames – The War Story of Southend Pier,** Southend County Borough Council, Southend Pier Museum.

Pattern, Marguerite, 1995, **The Victory Cookbook,** Imperial War Museum,

www.ingramcontent.com/pod-product-compliance
Lightning Source LLC
Chambersburg PA
CBHW022108090426
42743CB00008B/767